INFORMATION DESIGN

The Knowledge Architect's Toolkit

Graziella Tonfoni

The Scarecrow Press, Inc.
Lanham, Md.

intellect
Exeter, England

1998

SCARECROW PRESS, INC.

Published in the United States of America
by Scarecrow Press, Inc.
4720 Boston Way
Lanham, Maryland 20706

Published in Great Britain by
intellect
School of Art and Design,
Earl Richards Road North,
Exeter EX2 6AS
United Kingdom

ISBN 1-871516-61-7

British Library Cataloguing in Publication Information Available

Library of Congress Cataloging-in-Publication Data

Tonfoni, Graziella.
    Information design : the knowledge architect's toolkit / Graziella
Tonfoni.
        p.   cm.
    Includes index.
    ISBN 0-8108-3525-8 (cloth : alk. paper). — ISBN 0-8108-3526-6
(paper : alk. paper)
    1. Communication—Philosophy.   2. Communication models.
I. Title.
P90.T65   1998
302.2′01—dc21   98-21017
                                                            CIP

♾™ The paper used in this publication meets the minimum requirements of American
National Standard for Information Sciences—Permanence of Paper for Printed Library
Materials, ANSI Z39.48–1984. Manufactured in the United States of America.

Contents

The Knowledge Architect's Toolkit
Reading Map

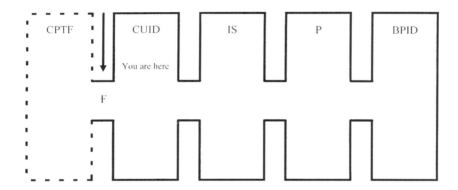

LEGEND:

CPTF = Communications Patterns and Textual Forms
F = Foreword
CUID = Context for Understanding Information Design
IS = Information States
P = Photographs
BPID = Basic Principles of Information Design

Foreword

Travellers who enter the information universe are seeking information. In order to find their way, they need maps, guides to existing information territories, and wayfinding instructions when no maps or guides exist. Travellers differ in the area they wish to explore, in their level of sophistication as travellers, in their understanding of the territory, and in their ability to reach their destination in a timely fashion. That destination is most likely a place where the desired information resides.

Tonfoni provides rules to guide us in reaching those information places. She also provides rules for designing a variety of information places and for understanding the elements of the design.

She asks, "what is the real meaning of the text in which information resides and once known, how does the information designer make this meaning evident?" She sees documents as constructions that can be stripped to their basic elements and then redesigned and reconstructed to meet specific information needs. Sometimes the document under consideration has previously been revised and the meaning changed so that the meaning is now unclear. In other instances, additional information has been added until the original structure and the meaning of the document is hidden.

She has formulated a number of rules which assist in clarifying the meaning of text and has designed a set of symbols which can be used to describe the content of the text. Is it a description, an opinion piece? How does it relate to other texts on the same or similar subject? New, highly specific, and highly analytic ways of looking at text and how it can be presented are described.

After being exposed to her ideas and their explication, one will never look at text in the same way. No longer will text be seen as words alone; a whole set of abstractions will make themselves known. In this process of discovering new abstractions and new relationships, new information territories may be discovered.

Her "Information States" presents a series of metaphors for approaching text. Place yourself in the role of the information traveller, select Tonfoni as the navigator, and take a trip or number of trips through the metaphorical information environments she has created. You may find yourself in a state in which text is seen as a complex architectural structure with separate but interdependent parts. Or you may find yourself in a dynamic environment in which information is ever changing and one finds it difficult to capture meaning. In another state, different information components are processed differently in order to capture different layers or textures of meaning. Additional "Information States" present further metaphors to help us understand how text changes both in the ways in which content is presented and in the ways in which it is or can be customized for the use and the user.

Analyzing text in new ways and designing text for specific purposes is a very complex task. Tonfoni has indicated that, just as an architect prepares plans for the construction of a building according to precise rules, information design also requires precise rules that must be followed precisely. In this way there is a common understanding of the tasks performed and there is the ability to replicate the task on the same or similar texts.

This is not an easy read, as new concepts and new and deeper ways of looking at and thinking about text are presented. Stay with it and the rewards are high. As a traveller in the information universe, one will begin to find guides, maps, and signposts to show the way and to describe what one finds.

Ann Prentice, Dean
College of Library
    and Information Services
Univeresity of Maryland
December 1, 1997

Preface

This book was conceived in Washington, D.C. Though it is a natural outgrowth of *Communicative Patterns and Textual Forms* (1996) in terms of the content and expansion of concepts I first illustrated in that book, the metaphorical environments I describe here are located in this city. It was in Washington where I started to feel a strong need to convey the completely absorbing experience I went through as a writer and researcher while conceiving and designing my theory and building consistent tools to be used for observation.

The need to lecture about some of the same chapters I was conceiving and to write them with the flavor of the lecturer who thinks of them as being delivered before an audience was triggered by the same intent that determined the famous book by Richard Feynmann, *Six Easy Pieces.* He expressed the strong belief that science may be enjoyable and conveyed through a set of lectures meant to reach a wider audience without losing their intensity and intent. This consideration refers to those chapters, which constitute the "Information States" section of this book.

In the process of writing these chapters, I was conceiving of them as being read aloud, performed, and enjoyed as a scientific journey, allowing the reader to grasp new scientific concepts and enjoy them through a pleasurable reading experience.

This has been my motivation and I hope the reader will recognize it between the lines.

The final section is based on visuals and schemes to be progressively filled up by the reader and are meant to facilitate active learning of these concepts, which were previously introduced.

It is therefore formatted so as to encourage each reader to create meaningful files, reorganizing the pages and renumbering them in a personalized way.

Acknowledgments

When I write, especially on innovative matters, I intentionally do a lot of handwriting and schemedrawing by hand first, therefore generating a very diversified amount of material to be then put together. Because I work this way, the final packaging of this book in a relatively short timespan would not have been possible without the substantial encouragement and technical support provided at The College of Library and Information Services at the University of Maryland, College Park, while I was a visiting professor in Information Design.

I am first of all most grateful to Dean Ann Prentice, who not only grasped immediately the meaning of my research efforts with her accurate listening, understanding, and sensitivity but also directly encouraged me into the enterprise. She finally wrote the foreword and did extremely careful reading of my English, making most relevant comments. Dr. Diane Barlow, assistant to the dean, supported me initially by creating the conditions for my book to be actually timely edited. Lindsy Gardner patiently and expertly retyped the IS section of my book, making sure that all the style revisions were properly incorporated within the text. Karen Patterson, director at IRS, always managed to provide most timely and appropriate and valuable technical support: I always knew I could count on her.

Norman Davis, computer technician at IRS, was always supportive with his skilled expertise, for any kind of question or need which may arise with the technologies used to produce the book. Jeanie Phillips, graduate assistant at IDS, supervised the technical reproduction of figures and schemes, which I had all previously handwritten and drawn by hand, and Debra Selby reproduced my figures with high sensitivity and accuracy, accompanying me and my book throughout the different stages of revision as to make it look the way it is now. I greatly appreciated her most valuable assistance.

This book represents ideas I explained during a series of special lectures to the faculty at CLIS, and I am indebted to my colleagues who have honored me with their presence and their accurate listening to my new theories and methodologies. I am particularly thankful for relevant remarks made to professor Gary Marchionini, always open to my ideas and most perceptive, and professors Bruce Dearstyne, Dagobert Soergel, James Liesener, Delia Neuman, Claude Walston and Doug Oard and then to Guido Francescato and Martin Gannon and Michael Clarke. I was also glad to have at my lectures graduate students Anita Komlodi, Tony Tse, Laura Slaughter, Paula Strain, Wei Ding, and Karla Hahn; due to their help all of my lectures could be profitably videotaped and are now available.

I want to thank Davide Zangara, my former student in computer science at the University of Bologna, now working at CIRFID, for accurately reproducing my handmade drawings regarding the IS section.

Special thanks are also due to Dr. Pete Daniel, curator of The National Museum of American History, Smithsonian Institution, for his care and friendship and supportive presence.

Special thanks also to Masoud Yazdani and Marvin Minshy for their support of my work, especially the material in Chapter 1.

A special acknowledgment for his continuous trust and most valuable encouragement is due to Edward Hill, former Technical Information Manager for the U.S. Navy, whose enthusiasm has been a tremendous support for me.

Last but not least: showing Chris Ehrmann how I would like him to take pictures around D.C. and have him so responsive to my requests has been a very positive experience altogether.

1

Context for Understanding Information Design

Introduction

This section presents basic criteria to define the field of information design. It also illustrates the need for metaphorical reasoning to organize wide information territories and turn them into "consistently functionalized knowledge buildings" and proposes cognitive tools for accurate interpretation. The overall theoretical framework presenting information design as "textual architecturing" based on physical laws of information is presented, along with some basic principles of information cartography. A distinction between micro information design problems and macro information design issues is drawn to distinguish among different kinds of concerns. Micro information design is the branch of information-processing concerned with individual information units and knowledge packages, whereas macro information design is concerned with the behavior of aggregate information variables through the study of information activities and processes taken as an interdependent and interconnected whole and represented as dynamic entities in their differentiated stages.

Information design is meant to be a science that analyzes allocation and utilization of information resources although most choices are made without the complete data spectrum available. Due to time and cost concerns, choices are therefore made based on projection and prediction. When organizing teaching material for developing skills in information design, the first step is to define the field to see how it may be integrated with related areas of expertise and research and such curricula as those in technical communication or human-computer interaction. Extremely valuable and highly specialized research already available (Sless 1978; Marchionini 1995; Schriver 1997) is aimed toward addressing such issues as information-seeking and describing criteria for designing manuals for instructions or software packages meant to

1

support the learning process and test the validity of the result. There is a need, however, to develop a broader vision of information and ways to develop sensitivity among the individual learners to the information to be processed. Only in this way will it be possible to convert information into highly functionalized knowledge buildings easily accessible to users. What is needed is a way to analyze the information to be processed along with the users' needs and the specific communicative context (Friedman 1997). The final goal is to provide information designers with both theoretical models and practical tools.

Packaging information to promote knowledge acquisition is a particularly delicate task. Attention must be paid to different cognitive profiles and cognitive attitudes of learners. Some redundancy and repetition may be useful to guarantee that no one is left behind.

If repetition is well planned and a topic is presented through the use of different codes harmoniously combined or alternating, learners will be offered the unique opportunity to acquire knowledge and learn about different packaging modes through which the same knowledge may be processed to be effectively conveyed. Style continuity will be an extremely helpful device for packaging knowledge to be acquired for the first time. To ensure that the same knowledge has been acquired, nothing may work better than multiple repackaging of the same body of knowledge.

An information designer needs to be able to plan consistently and to organize knowledge buildings as well as information territories and open spaces. Sensitivity to information matter to be processed and to information coming in different states, such as natural language, icons, or visual languages at different levels of complexity, must be developed by anyone in the field.

Just as architectural studies entails some physics, especially regarding basic physical principles and laws regulating the construction process, and some chemistry, especially regarding properties of the material used in the building process, an information design course must include basic principles of text construction to develop in students an awareness of the physical laws of communicative equilibrium and balancing between and among different codes being used. Architectural studies also entails learning about the presentation and choice of a wide set of examples of styles developed by architects to promote interpretation skills about types of buildings, according to different perspectives and building ideologies adopted throughout the construction process (Salvadori 1980; Levi and Salvadori 1987). In the same way, a course in information design should include the current literature of texts, manuals, and software inspired by different constructing criteria (Tufte 1990; Tufte 1991). If knowledge of current literature in the field and different perspectives, styles, and personalities within the information design tradition is important, consistent parallel development of context sensitivity and awareness about the users' needs should be addressed at the same time. These learning tracks will develop students' ability to plan and design information at a global level.

The individual teacher's style and personality will inevitably influence the overall perspective, giving rise to a wide range of different and highly recognizable ways of structuring knowledge. Similarly, in painting Tintoretto created a "scuola" of students who, inspired by his influence, painted in a way different from any others. In designing information and creating an architecture of knowledge, a solid and comprehensive theoretical framework will reflect cognitively sound ways of designing, planning, and building information. Both theories of text comprehension and of text compression (Tonfoni 1989–94; Tonfoni 1995) may be viewed as ways to share a vocabulary for defining operations to be performed upon text during the text construction process—just as blueprints are meant to convey the architect's plans to a crew of carpenters and workers to facilitate interaction and a group mentality aimed toward completion of a complex task.

Information design should not be limited to text processing: flows of information work in fact in very complex, dynamic, and discontinuous ways. Any knowledge architect will therefore have to maintain his or her vision and perspective over the complexity of each task. This is precisely where and how the need for a multilayered analysis comes in, together with the need to develop competence in working through analogies and metaphors. Analogical reasoning is an extremely valuable cognitive tool, meant to facilitate information organization through a more global vision of complex and dynamic problems (Hollis 1994). The process of designing metaphors will entail precise rules and principles such as accuracy, visibility, range of application, relevant features selection, progression, approximation, consistency, and continuity. Information design as an evolving process of thinking and rethinking must be based on accurate vision of information flows and, in a much broader sense, of organizing a whole information territory with different tools, functions, and kinds of material.

High sensitivity is also needed regarding the information to be processed into stabilized knowledge that satisfies conditions of easiness, lightness, insulation, and resistance. Accurate rethinking of changes involved in the process of writing in different media is one of the first issues to be addressed. Multimedia writing, for example, which means packaging information for Web pages, should not be the same kind of writing as for a newspaper or for books: it should rather be tailored to computer-triggered text visualization and perception. A rethinking of such cognitive processes as focusing, selecting, and balancing between the visual and linguistic codes is therefore needed for accurate planning. Transporting information from books, papers, and videos to a Web page requires complex skills for appropriate and cognitively sound reconfiguration. A course in information design should create sensitivity to the specific context (Perkins 1994), the nature of the information to be packaged, and the kind of information access to be supported.

Metaphorical Reasoning for Designing Information

Because complexity is so difficult to handle anyway, natural language will be most useful for referring to a highly articulated framework for interpretation of the different states of information. Introducing new conceptual tools to interpret newly observed phenomena will trigger the need for an "in-depth search" within new metaphorical realms, which have been defined as metaphorical environments (Tonfoni 1997), and are meant to support dynamic reasoning about communication both quantitatively and qualitatively. Applying metaphors to information design means creating a conceptual platform for supporting newly defined concepts with derivative experience coming from other fields that are well known. Such a process may be of tremendous assistance in facilitating reasoning, once the interpretation perspective and point of view have been accurately defined. A commonly shared metaphorical environment is also an important support for an overall rethinking of communication among individuals involved with collective and cooperative tasks performance.

Accurate rethinking of the inner nature of information and consistent redefinition of communicative interactions by introducing physical models of reasoning and by proposing and building metaphorical environments for taking action are in fact fundamental steps toward better coordination of any information-seeking, filtering, interpreting, and filing process, both by individuals and groups of individuals acting cooperatively. "Information" is such a general and abstract term that any specific analogy drawn from physical models may contribute significantly to the overall interpretation. Accurate observation and interpretation of complex situations through precisely defined metaphors and metaphorical environments will lead not just researchers but everyone who is interested into a deeper understanding and mastery of complex situations and an effective interpretation process. Experts will be able therefore to undertake collective action and share the overall framework for interpretation.

Planning and refining the design of a consistent metaphorical environment will result in an extremely delicate operation, which implies a previous selection process and consistent reinterpretation of relevant aspects. A global reconfiguration of elements relevant to being transferred from one well-known domain into a new one is needed. Words should not be taken for granted, nor should ways to express concepts and explain processes be considered obvious just because they sound familiar. Consequently, each term needs to be reframed and redefined; without such a progressively organized reconceptualization process, fuzziness and confusion may arise. Entering a specific metaphorical environment may therefore mean something close to entering a reconstruction of a living and housing situation within an exhibit, showing and explaining through material tools and objects the inner nature of life in another cultural setting, in a different age, or both. Though we may enter such an environment with some knowledge and expectations about what we are likely to find, in order to actually capture the meaning of such a recreated metaphorical environment, we must be open to accurate observation of the exhibited tools and objects as well as to a consistent reinterpretation of their function and value in their actual setting. Only by being open to an in-depth perception of such interpretation cues will we be able to gain an accurate understanding as opposed to a set of merely superficial impressions.

In order to really grasp the essence of what we are exposed to, we must rid ourselves of "prejudiced knowledge" about what we may already think an object is for or a certain word means. Such expectations may in fact close up possibilities for new information and knowledge to be organized and acquired. This is a preliminary and crucial step for acquiring in-depth understanding of any scientific metaphor or metaphorical environment meant to promote incremental learning about new concepts based on a previously known conceptual platform. Information design metaphors need to be based on accurate extraction and transfer of relevant features from one well-known domain, like architectural studies, toward a new domain to be progressively defined. Just as a sculpture could never express anything not already possible in the material, the same principle applies to the planning of a metaphorical environment for information design and the progressive shaping of meaning.

The very first step is to get rid of consolidated semantics so as to be able to work out the details, polishing, and sharpening of new concepts and procedures. Just as different tools may be created to facilitate performance of a certain task and some may turn out to be better than others, the same conceptual tool may be used in different ways and at different levels and some may turn out to be more effective than others. If there are different degrees of approximation in performing a certain task, there are also different levels of approximation in grasping the essence of the task itself through the use of different kinds of metaphors in a progressive combination. More than that, the same metaphor may be used at different ranks of accuracy or fuzziness. Just as a craftsman must work out the planning details according to some previous design and through different stages to have the final product reflect the model, the information designer must be aware of all the details to be worked out in advance to have the resulting metaphor or metaphorical environment reflect the highest possible degree of accuracy of the plan. What a metaphorical environment may make visible, and therefore intelligible and easier to understand, is the result of a whole set of selection and abstraction processes that have been activated by the information designer. Complexity is a substantial part of the planning, designing, and organizing of wide information territories and knowledge buildings. A metaphorical environment is dynamic by nature and well suited to show the complexity of information design problems and tasks that need to be represented both analytically and synthetically.

A metaphor may be defined as the result of transferring a certain meaning from relevant features in a well-established and well-known domain into a new and not so well established (because unknown or still vaguely described) domain. The transferred meaning may be just one connotative or denotative element or an entire concept or chain of concepts. It is well known that a metaphor in poetry not only allows but welcomes a whole set of possible interpretations and is therefore meant to be "centrifugal," which means that its definition is based upon multiple meanings. To make sure that each metaphor used for designing information is precise—in the sense of conveying specifically those features intended to be conveyed—such a metaphor will need to be "centripetal," meaning that its definition should be based upon a precise definition or set of consistent definitions.

A metaphor is usually generated within a certain realm, which means that it comes from a certain region of meaning where different semantic attributions may occur and some may alternatively prevail or dominate. Metaphorical perception in poetry is based upon the most appropriate co-occurrences of various meanings. The same concept may not be reproduced in the design of information, which must utilize highly specific meaning attribution to avoid undesired fuzziness. In order to become both reliable and effective for designing information, any metaphor will have to be conceived as part of a more global conceptual framework, based upon a skeletal structure of meaning that has previously been designed, set up, and shown in a detailed representation with its parts joined together. Only at this point will the skilled and sensitive information designer be able to proceed toward an accurate and highly specific definition of each part. And only at this point will the metaphorical domain be ready to be turned into an operative tool for interpretation and understanding of a complex phenomenon, becoming a more global metaphorical environment within which a whole set of information problems may be analyzed in their dynamic and multidimensional perspective.

Before getting into a more accurate definition of an operationally valid metaphorical environment, let us briefly go back to the process whereby any metaphor for designing information must evolve. In order to undergo significant changes, the metaphor will change status progressively, proceeding toward different stages that may resemble transformations occurring when a concept is transferred from a "plenum of meaning" into a "vacuum of meaning." "Plenum of meaning" is a state or space in which an element is contained at a meaning attribution pressure that is greater than actual contextual and desired meaning attribution pressure (Tonfoni 1997). Because the whole interpretation space is filled with semantic matter and previous and undesired semantic accretion may jeopardize new contextual meaning attribution, a filtering process must be used to reduce the level of fuzziness. A vacuum of meaning is a desirable situation to be reached progressively; it is an enclosed interpretation space from which undesired contextual accretion has been more or less removed, so that semantic matter remaining in the interpretation space will exert less pressure than the actually desired contextual attribution. This is the opposite of what we would see within a plenum. A vacuum of meaning represents the state of lowest semantic energy and contextual attribution possible. Only after a condition of vacuum has been reached may an accurately planned metaphorical domain be productively turned into an operationally valid metaphorical environment for information design. If a vacuum condition has not yet been reached, any metaphor not having undergone the filtering process will carry undesired contextual accretion and fuzziness.

Within an appropriately constructed metaphorical environment for information design, each of the components is so precisely defined in its own meaning, function, and range of applications as to be interpreted both consistently and consensually. Only after such an accurate definition based on rethinking and reframing processes has occurred will the environment be properly defined as the aggregate of surrounding conditions or influences for making qualitative reasoning about communication possible. As a consequence of a shared core of precisely defined concepts, the metaphorical environment for designing information will be turned into an operational model, according to which kinds of processes are made possible and understandable.

To represent complex problems first and solve them next, a combination of different metaphors may work both at a higher speed and at a higher degree of precision and reliability. A metaphor may grasp just some aspects of a certain domain, whereas a different metaphor may grasp some others that would otherwise be missing or left out. As communication is such a complex realm, only a kaleidoscopic combination of different models for visualizing and expressing various aspects of the same problem could possibly map such complexity. This way, we may distinguish between large-scale metaphors and reduced-scale metaphors, and between operational metaphors and narrative metaphors, so as to accurately evaluate the degree of approximation they may reach. What cannot be captured by just one model may be well interpreted by a new and different one, without contradicting the previous one, just as a political map of a territory does not contradict a geographical one but rather addresses different issues and focuses on different features. Most important is the clarity and sharpness needed to identify those relevant features, which must first be made to surface and then to be visualized and represented.

Textual Architecture and Textual Cartography

Architecture may be viewed as a whole metaphorical environment meant to open up the possibility for interpreting text as an evolving construction and for conceiving natural language text production as the result of macro and micro design processes. Text will need to be planned and accurately conceived as to be consistently organized; more accurate planning will result in a highly functionalized construction.

Architecture is defined in the Random House dictionary as "the profession of designing buildings, open areas and other artificial constructions and environments, usually with some regard to aesthetic effect. Architecture often includes design or selection of furnishings and decorations, supervision of construction work and the examination, restoration or remodeling of existing buildings." Textual architecture will also cover a whole set of activities, ranging from the design of highly functionalized texts, to accurate definition of open spaces for information flows, to text decoration, restoration, and remodeling. Reframing such concepts leads toward a better and more effective way to reformulate operations, which are very distinct but, if not observed and carefully defined, may look mixed and quite fuzzy altogether.

Architects use planning and design as a fundamental precondition for activating and monitoring the building process performed by teams, and they share a terminology to enable them to communicate what they are proposing and supervise the construction. Similarly, precise terminology must be used consensually to name different operations to be performed upon text, both synchronously and asynchronously. In architecture there are also precise laws to be respected and constraints due to the material used; however, personal styles may be developed and recognized. The same happens in the construction of texts, which may be built in different languages and through different and personal styles, but all reside on strongly grounded principles of communication and laws of cognitive balance. Reframing the overall organization of a text in terms of balancing between laws of construction and possibilities of variation seems to reflect the complexity of the task itself.

The architect must be a scientist, aware of those physical laws affecting the construction as well as of chemical properties of the material; a skilled technician, able to use specifically acquired expertise; and an artist, able to approximate through accurate design the ideal model. Tension between real and objective constraints and idealized models to be implemented represents the fundamental condition for any construction.

There is absolutely no doubt that information design and knowledge mapping, which may also be thought of as a form of textual cartography including texts, images, commentaries, etc., will affect and shape society significantly and not just on a short-term basis. Information designers today are knowledge architects. They have to face both challenge and responsibility for mapping vast information territories that must survive and progressively expand. Any topographical model is based upon a certain geographic theory, and mapping may result in significantly different models of representation whether based on a Ptolemaic system of reference, a Newtonian one, or a Copernican one

(Biddle, Milne, and Shortle 1974). In accurate mapping of information, not only is it crucial to make an early decision about the amount of information to be represented, but it is also extremely important to rely upon a theory behind what is being represented, so as to be able to proceed toward planning and design. Just as geographic maps may represent different aspects of the same land, information maps must be designed consistently with what they are meant to convey, according to different possible users' modes of navigation according to different purposes. Just as geographical maps reflect the technological level of a society and its knowledge and perception of the world, in the same way information maps will reflect very precise kinds of interpretation through new technological tools and by means of new theories that open up the possibility of seeing what was invisible before.

Textual maps are therefore conceived as derivative texts out of an originating text, having undergone a certain process or a set of processes. Just like maps, they are intended to be used for some specific purposes, therefore representing symbolic and reduced versions of the text from which they have been derived. As such, they work on a quantitatively reduced text, which results in a qualitatively enhanced model of the text itself.

A textual map is not only conceived as a reproduction of the text to be represented, but will result in a manageable abstraction of the spatial distribution of information, helping to eliminate noise and distortion within the mapping system both on the mapmaker's and the map user's side. In mapping texts, just as in mapping territories, it is most important to make sure that the "channel capacity" does not become saturated with too many details or noise. This means precisely if mapping is too dense with information, the reader may become overwhelmed and lose or lower significantly the interpretation capacities and active reactions to new information.

Some noise in textual mapping may also derive from addition of information that may not be relevant to the map's function. Some noise may be generated by the textual map designer and may be reduced significantly in the course of accurate revision processes. A textual map is therefore a symbolic representation of a text that reflects and indicates precisely those properties the textual map designer perceives as most fundamental within a certain text and therefore must be the essential ones to be highlighted, according to a consistent and agreed-upon model that has been planned explicitly to help the map reader. Any textual map will of course reduce the actual text in very precisely defined and highly selective ways, just as scales in maps do. Such abbreviation will therefore impose other specific constraints on use and further interpretation of the originating and consistently mapped text.

A model is an interpretative device meant to help understand a more or less complex system. The more complex the system, the more articulated the model will be; statically designed models may have to be turned into dynamic ones to show aspects that would otherwise be missing. Linear representation systems may have to become three-dimensional to express aspects that would otherwise be lost, and many levels of complexity observed and identified may have to be turned into three-layered representation systems to be fully exploited. Textual maps and other textual models are strictly dependent upon the actual text they are planned to represent. Meanwhile, they also must produce a breakthrough and provide a deeper understanding of each text, which has been previously analyzed and processed, in order to identify which kind of noise needs to be removed. What is highly significant versus what is disturbing noise depends upon the kind of texts being investigated, the problems that have been previously addressed, and the personal judgment of each investigator. Like any model referring to a continuously changing and expanding reality, the effectiveness of textual maps will change over time according to new information.

Textual maps, just like well-designed models, may be predictive in the sense that they may be used as a basis for decision making and planning of new texts, though many variables may be left out. Textual maps do in fact consistently summarize selected information about the originating text in a highly structured way, therefore suggesting new paths for further investigation of texts within a certain knowledge domain that has been previously identified and consistently mapped. Textual mapping is not only appropriate at a descriptive level, but also at an operational level: consistency of the model will guarantee that the results that had been planned originally may be obtained. A specific competence based upon a combination of skills needs to be developed in order to be able to perform those tasks that have been synthetically described.

On Designing Manuals for Information Design

It is hard to think and plan with no physical models available. This is why selection of relevant models is so important as to be able to recognize and name processes that would otherwise be very hard to discover and would therefore remain unknown. Information design is based both on "visualizing" and on "envisioning" capabilities. To be able to visualize some aspects of linguistic communication, a whole set of physical models of reasoning about natural language may be found in Tonfoni 1989–94, 95. In order to envision complex and dynamic flows of information, highly articulated architectural structures will be needed in the reader's mind to support construction of metaphorical environments for rethinking, planning, and modeling as well as for solving highly complex and difficult communication issues.

Accurate design is based upon identification and solution of a set of relevant problems and upon a set of decision-making processes. Strategies and plans will only become effective after a sound description and representation of the problem to be solved has been produced. Information designers should acquire different kinds of skills and should know the possibilities and constraints of the different codes. Mixing and combining codes is a fundamental precondition for conveying different kinds of information. No such thing as unplanned and generic organization of information and knowledge should ever be pursued. Any knowledge construction should be carefully planned, according to the kind of function that has been previously assigned. It may in fact take a few books instead of just one as to really promote awareness in designing information for knowledge acquisition, as it shows in figures 1.1–1.4, respectively. (For more accurate explanation see: http://www.intellect-net.com/authors/tonfoni.htm.) Attention must be paid to different cognitive profiles and cognitive attitudes of learners (although some "productive redundancy" is welcome) to guarantee that nothing is left out. If some repetition is well planned and a specific topic is presented at different times through different codes harmoniously combined or alternating, learners will be offered the unique opportunity to acquire knowledge and become aware of different ways the "same knowledge" may be conveyed. This approach reflects that of the architect, who knows that a building requires different kinds of material for completion of the overall project, according to different kinds of functions and priorities that have been set up. Style continuity is an extremely helpful device for packaging any kind of knowledge to be acquired for the first time.

To make sure that the same knowledge has been acquired, nothing may work better than a "multiple style multiple repackaging solution" meant to present content selected and prioritized, but in various and different forms. Offering different kinds of solutions at a second stage may result in a tremendously powerful way for "stabilizing" newly presented knowledge. It does take more time, but it is worth the effort at the end: The acquisition process will be not only activated, but effectively reinforced. Information territories and knowledge buildings represent effective metaphors for information design because they incorporate dynamic aspects of space and time and reproduce the process of organization, selection, and focusing according to a project evolving in different steps. The fact that information is to be continuously updated has created the need to think of information decay and information update and upgrade as crucial issues to be addressed. The consequences of permanent instability in acquiring information and the continuous need for change may in fact sometimes result in uncommitted behavior both on the part of knowledge producers and information users. Change needs therefore to be foreseen and integrated directly into the process of designing information territories and planning knowledge buildings in the form of maps and projections. Only in this way is it possible for learners to feel committed to the knowledge acquisition process, still being aware of where the information flow comes from and where and when it may be discontinued, or that it may be continued at some point, taking a different direction and a different form.

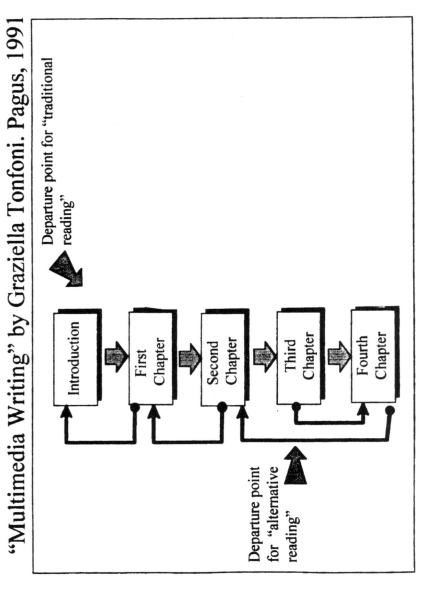

Figure 1.1. Multimedia writing. The Book Content Organization.

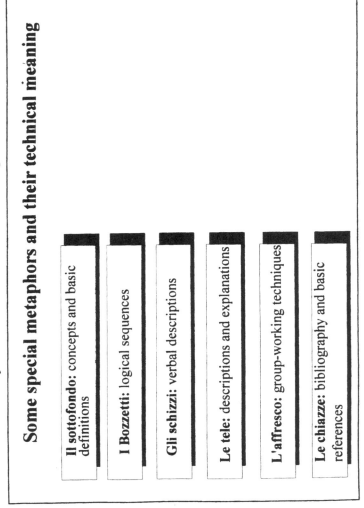

"Business Communication as Visual Art"
by Graziella Tonfoni. Pagus, 1992

Some special metaphors and their technical meaning

Il sottofondo: concepts and basic definitions

I Bozzetti: logical sequences

Gli schizzi: verbal descriptions

Le tele: descriptions and explanations

L'affresco: group-working techniques

Le chiazze: bibliography and basic references

Figure 1.2. Business communication as visual art. The Book Content Organization.

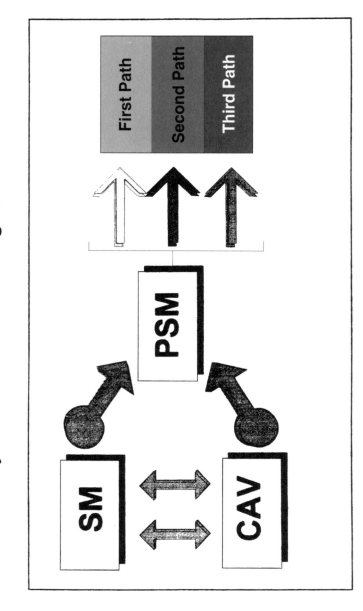

Figure 1.3. Partitioning, solfa, movement. The Book Content Organization.

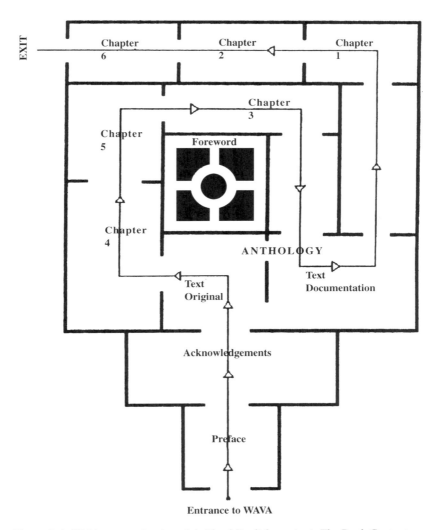

Figure 1.4. Writing as a visual art (abridged English version). The Book Content Organization. (Courtesy of Intellect©.)

Conclusions

Developing those kinds of multiple skills is one of the missions of a course in information design. There is no need to say that the way information-processing is organized deeply influences individuals' lives. The way information is designed today will in fact deeply affect people's learning processes and their ability to access knowledge in a very wide sense. This is the real challenge and responsibility for everyone in the field of information design.

2

Information States

Introduction

This section of the book follows from my book *Communication Patterns and Textual Forms* (Tonfoni 1996) and extends some of its chapters by reframing, redefining, and providing further specification to some of its main concepts. While that earlier book was meant for a diversified audience, this section is intended for an audience specifically interested in pursuing theoretical and practical development, evolution, and extension of theories of text comprehension (Tonfoni 1989–94) and text compression (Tonfoni 1995) and understanding their nature and purpose especially regarding information design.

The aim of my research has been to capture, analyze, and enlighten the complexity of information-processing and, more specifically, that "state of information" represented by natural language, and to do so within a systematically, consistently organized and highly articulated framework for interpretation. Because complexity is difficult to handle, I plan to facilitate the process with a set of consistently designed interpretive tools meant to be used both separately and in combination with each other.

The process of introducing new concepts triggers the need for a reconceptualization of both consistent and flexible metaphors and metaphorical realms, which will be defined here as "metaphorical environments." These are meant to support reasoning about communication on both a quantitative and a qualitative level.

Adopting and applying metaphors in science require the creation of a platform for supporting newly defined concepts with evidence and derivative experience from other fields. The process may be of tremendous assistance for facilitating reasoning about newly introduced concepts and categories, once the interpretation perspective and point of view have been shifted and more or less radically redefined. This creates a common metaphorical environment, which is a necessary support for collective rethinking and reorganizing of communication coordination.

Among individuals involved with collective task performance, accurate re-thinking of information structure and consistent redefinition of communicative interactions—both by introducing physical models of reasoning and by pro-posing and "building" metaphorical environments for taking action—seem to be a fundamental step toward better coordination of information-seeking, filtering, interpreting, and filing processes.

To develop satisfactory metaphorical environments to describe and explain coordinated communicative actions taking place in complex situations, I have first examined and tried to define my own way of working out theories and conducting research on natural language and communication. Once I under-stand the process of analyzing phenomena and comparing experiments, I will then be able to confront and compare results.

Accurate observation and interpretation of complex situations through con-sistent design of precisely defined metaphors and metaphorical environments will lead not just researchers in the field, but anyone interested, into a deeper understanding of complex situations. Moving in this way toward an effective interpretation process will therefore enable each individual to take action within a consensually shared framework for interpretation.

The planning and design of a consistent metaphorical environment consti-tutes an extremely delicate operation, which implies a selection among differ-ent possibilities, consistent reinterpretation of relevant aspects, and accurate reformulation of each item of a selected and precisely redefined lexicon. It also implies a consistent and more global reconfiguration of those aspects that are relevant in order to transfer them from one well-known domain into a new one, as well as to define to what extent and for what purpose they are being transferred. Words can not be taken for granted, nor can ways of expressing concepts and explaining processes be considered obvious, just because they resemble commonly used words or analogous situations occurring in different domains. Consequently, each term needs to be accurately reframed and rede-fined. Without such a previous and progressively organized reconceptualiza-tion, fuzziness and confusion may arise later, jeopardizing the final result.

The construction of a metaphorical environment may be compared to the discovery of a mathematical algorithm, requiring a high degree of accuracy and precision to be profitably used. Entering a metaphorical environment may approximate the experience of entering a constructed exhibit that uses material tools and objects to demonstrate life in another cultural setting or a different age. Though we may enter such an environment with previous knowledge and some expectations about what we may find there, in order to actually capture the meaning and real flavor of such a recreated environment, we must closely observe the exhibited tools and objects while accepting a consistent reinterpre-tation of their function and value in their actual setting. Only by being open to such in-depth perception can we really gain an accurate understanding, as opposed to a set of superficial and vague impressions.

In order to really learn and grasp the essence of what we are being exposed to, we must first push aside "prejudiced knowledge" about what we may already think an object is for or a word means. Such expectations may in fact deny the possibilities of acquiring new information and discovering new ways to organize knowledge. This is therefore a preliminary and crucial step for gaining "in-depth understanding" of any scientific metaphor and metaphorical environment meant to promote incremental learning about new concepts, for it requires moving away from a previously known and well-established conceptual platform.

Scientific metaphors are, in fact, based on accurate extraction and transfer of relevant features from one domain, which is well known, to a new domain where they can be progressively defined and properly interpreted. Just as a sculpture can not convey anything that was not already possible in the material (Michelangelo described the creation of sculpture as a process of "taking away"), the same can be said about the creation of a metaphorical environment and the progressive shaping of meaning by progressively and systematically eliminating consolidated semantics so as to work out the details, i.e., "polishing" and "sharpening" the newly acquired meaning in all its significance and strength.

Just as different tools may be created to perform a certain task and some may turn out to be better than others, even the same tool may be used in different ways and at different levels, some of which may be more effective than others. If there are indeed different degrees of approximation in performing a certain task, there are also different levels of approximation in grasping the essence of the task itself. Through the use of various kinds of metaphors in a progressive combination, the same metaphor may also be used at different levels of accuracy or approximation.

Just as a craftsman shapes the details of an object according to some previous design to reflect the ideal, the scientific metaphor designer and scientist must work out all the necessary details to make the resulting metaphor or metaphorical environment really represent and reflect, to the highest possible degree of accuracy, what was meant when it was first planned. Vaguely designed metaphors may add fuzziness rather than enhancing understanding, just as an ill-defined or imprecise metaphor may produce confusion and misunderstanding. What a well-designed metaphorical environment makes visible, intelligible, and easier to understand is the result of a lot of work done previously, incorporating a lot of complexity in the process of planning and design.

This book is therefore designed to illustrate and accurately explain seven major metaphorical environments for information design. It is also meant to demonstrate how analogical thinking and qualitative reasoning may be applied to the resolution of highly complex problems in information planning, modelling, and organizing.

A lexicon of newly introduced terminology is also provided to assure a shared understanding of different processes and actions to be performed on texts. Before beginning a detailed presentation of each metaphorical environment, an illustration of a metaphorical laboratory for the physics of language and the chemistry of information will be presented to show how theories of text comprehension and text compression have evolved.

The Physics of Language and Chemistry of the Information Laboratory

When I first started thinking about creating a "new" theory and a different "perspective" for interpreting information and communication via natural language, I first addressed the issues of what was available, which tools for observation were needed for those kinds of problems, and which could be considered relevant to a solution. Because I certainly was not the first researcher to address the issue of language complexity from a scientific point of view, my first move was to see what other researchers in this and related fields could provide both for reference and practical use.

The object of observation—the material to be analyzed—had to be texts of different kinds having different purposes and being of different sizes. They could be either in a "volatile" spoken format or in a "more stabilized" written format. It was evident, from the beginning, that available theories were intended to address specific problems about detailed aspects of language, in the sense of exploring the variety of existing spoken languages.

To produce accurate descriptions of each language under observation, a set of very specific phenomena had first to be isolated and then accurately analyzed in order to proceed toward a consistent and reliable explanation, according to a predefined set of parameters and criteria. Each theory should be measured and evaluated against these criteria for its reliability and explanatory power.

Some continuity between the need to adopt a certain theory and the mode of observation triggered by the theory itself directly reflects observed phenomena and those selected relevant features. These must be considered to constitute the effective domain for observation.

It is clear that any researcher must make a whole set of choices and decisions and establish some continuity with respect to any previous research driven by either the same or highly compatible principles. This is how knowledge within a scientific field increases incrementally: It just keeps growing and moving along a certain predefined path or it becomes momentarily independent and creates new output results. Once proved in their own validity, these new results are then brought back to the original field, after having been accurately checked and tested according to newly established and well-defined evaluation criteria.

Referring to linguistics *stricto sensu* (that is, among an innumerable set of contributions made to the observation and description of a variety of qualitatively different phenomena surfacing in various languages at different levels), the first scientific approach to language interpretation was Noam Chomsky's *Syntactic Structures* in 1957.

As with any scientific framework, Chomsky's model has undergone major changes, mostly while the core system for interpreting and explaining language was confronting the variety of specific languages. These had been designed to justify and explain at the syntactic level why one is chosen to be observed, described, and justified. Trials and revisions represent evolving stages of a theory, which is explicitly designed to be applied to bodies of languages that are "alive," meaning they are subject to change and are dynamically evolving. Consistent with his preliminary choice, Chomsky used biology and genetics to create a metaphorical environment aimed at explaining the "syntactic behaviour" of natural languages.

For myself, confronting communicative aspects of natural language in their respective complexity means first defining semantic and pragmatic problems to be handled with a variety of highly specific conceptual tools.

The most obvious direction for further exploration is research on the mind occurring in the fields of cognitive science and artificial intelligence. Among the theories available, Minsky's approach, described in his *The Society of Mind* in 1986, proved of tremendous help for gaining insight into the mind through an extremely articulated metaphorical environment meant to support further research with a set of consistently and precisely redefined terms. More generally, research in the field of knowledge representation proved to be an extremely valuable support for rethinking and consistently reframing models of reasoning via natural language. Clearly current models for knowledge representation (Minsky 1975; Schank 1980; Lehnert 1981; Wilensky 1983) are addressing a set of relevant issues even if they are not meant to be operating at the same level. However, the target of my research was the construction of a metaphorical environment meant to model, organize, and reframe those information-packaging modes that reflect and show through natural language as a consequence of precise cognitive processes that have been activated.

The long detour through research in knowledge representation returned me to considering which models of representation I should consistently reframe in order to trigger accurate rethinking of those language phenomena that had proved most relevant to be isolated, observed, and interpreted. Chomsky proceeded from the "bottom up," identifying the syntactic level as the relevant one to place under scientific observation and declaring "sentence" to be the primary entity to be analyzed. However, by claiming the "quantum nature" of language units, governed by energies, which may determine and polarize their contextual meaning according to the three-dimensional positioning of each, I proceeded "top down" and explicitly decided to refer to a different scientific paradigm for my exploration of language matter. My newly defined paradigm reflects basic assumptions of physics mostly and chemistry somehow.

The metaphorical environment, which I have chosen and organized with the specific intent of representing, explaining, and justifying strong claims made at a theoretical level, is also meant to facilitate an in-depth understanding of those tools I have conceived, designed, and tested to turn them into both accurate scientific devices for observation and handy tools for practical use. Within the "laboratory" metaphorical environment, I intend to create evidence for the study of the physics of language. This first implies being able to identify those universally valid energies and forces that are active upon natural language all the time. By "identify," I mean I have made them visible through the design of models constructed to represent them both statically and dynamically. To make special reactions possible, I began by studying the inner nature of the chemistry of information, in order to analyze transformations and to foresee new combinations by using the tools for observation I had previously designed. Thus it became possible to perform highly distinct functions and diverse operations upon language.

Matter to be analyzed within the newly established framework is "language in context" in all its inherent complexity, but occurring primarily in the form of text that was selected as the basic unit of investigation and analysis. It was text or text segments that reflected the communicative positioning of individuals who had been producing those texts, though they appear together with the interferences and sedimentation of context and deeply affect the overall interpretation.

According to such a view, language is matter in different states, deeply influenced by concretions of previously assigned context attributions and cultural implications, but with a lot of fuzziness and inherent complexity deriving from such stratification. Control over such complexity, in this view, rests with individuals communicating via natural language only to the extent that they function by using specific tools for interpretation and monitoring, just as pilots perform complex, both synchronous and asynchronous operations at a control panel.

Through the preliminary definition of a set of highly specific conceptual tools, I have built a more general framework for operating text and monitoring the process of interpretation. As neither the speaker nor the writer may be totally in control of the understanding of the text, the hearer or reader may not think of optimizing intended interpretation unless it is clear for speaker, writer, hearer, and reader that they have to handle language matter. That matter has a lot of contextual accretion and contamination, which they will have to cope with by analyzing the different layers with specifically designed tools.

The "power" of communication resides therefore in the hands of both communicative partners, who will be sharing a set of tools in order to consensually control and monitor within an operational model, the communication flow. That flow will result in different information states.

Matter, to be properly understood, must be observed and explored with appropriately devised tools and at different stages. Close connections may be shown with scientific observation of physical elements in different stages and various chemical compositions. In chemistry, Kirchhoff showed Bunsen that instead of looking through colored glass to distinguish between similarly colored flames, he could use a prism to separate the light into its constituent rays. Using that principle, they developed the spectroscope, an instrument that proved of supreme importance not only in chemical analysis but also in the discovery of new elements (Weeks-Leicester 1968). Continued experiments resulted in the identification of new and astonishing phenomena, and a simple method was found for separating newly observed compositions. Kirchhoff also found a new element, named it "cesium," and explored its atomic weight.

Carrying this analogy to language, I have used a battery of observational devices to isolate distinct elements that are linked together in language performance.

The departure point for observing communication facts and phenomena has been textual canvases and textual machines. These may therefore be used as a "textual spectroscope" to recognize and dynamically observe cognitive processes at play once a text has been analyzed. Figures 2.1 and 2.2 represent textual machines and textual canvases in CPP-TRS.

(CPP-TRS [Communicative Positioning Program-Text Representation Systems] was fully conceived, designed, and tested by Graziella Tonfoni. It is a highly articulated visual language based on a set of twelve textual canvases, meant to represent global action at a still "scruffy" level in the original planning of text; ten signs and fourteen symbols, meant to represent different functionalities to be exploited in various kinds of texts; and fifteen textual machines, which are dynamic and physical models representing different cognitive processes active while we write and read. A visual representation of multiple and complex aspects in text will trigger much deeper and consistent perception of both writing and reading processes. Enhancing perception and sensitivity about those "invisible" aspects of text will create awareness and consistently improve final performance.)

A detailed description of the CPP-TRS visual presented in this section may be found in Tonfoni (1995b, 1995c, 1996a, 1996b) and on the web page http://www.intellect-net.com/authors/tonfoni.htm

Textual canvases have been designed and used as a kind of "textual microscope" meant to enlighten very precise phenomena occurring in text. It is possible then to proceed toward designing and applying a "textual gridcase"

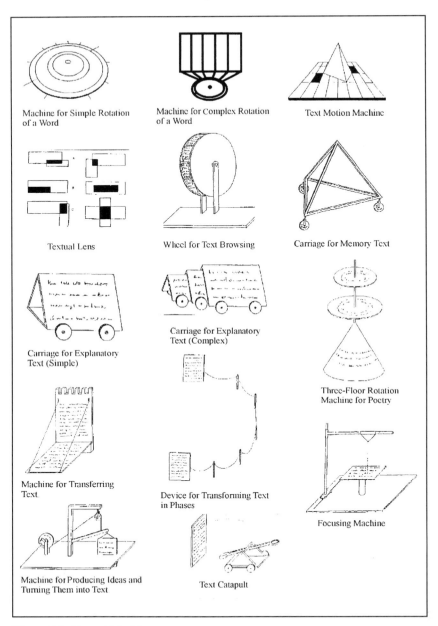

Machine for Simple Rotation
of a Word

Machine for Complex Rotation
of a Word

Text Motion Machine

Textual Lens

Wheel for Text Browsing

Carriage for Memory Text

Carriage for Explanatory
Text (Simple)

Carriage for Explanatory
Text (Complex)

Three-Floor Rotation
Machine for Poetry

Machine for Transferring
Text

Device for Transforming Text
in Phases

Focusing Machine

Machine for Producing Ideas and
Turning Them into Text

Text Catapult

Figure 2.1. Textual Machines.

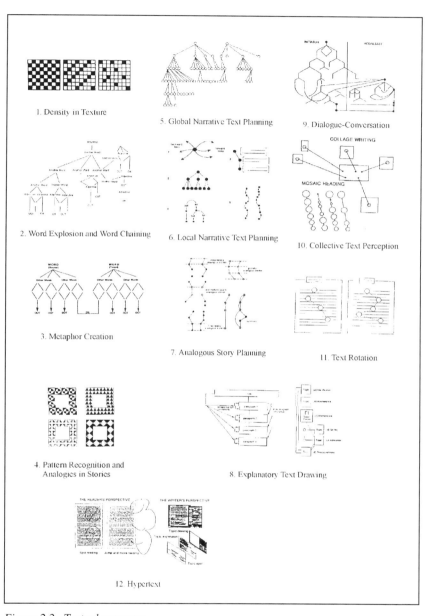

1. Density in Texture

2. Word Explosion and Word Chaining

3. Metaphor Creation

4. Pattern Recognition and Analogies in Stories

5. Global Narrative Text Planning

6. Local Narrative Text Planning

7. Analogous Story Planning

8. Explanatory Text Drawing

9. Dialogue-Conversation

10. Collective Text Perception

11. Text Rotation

12. Hypertext

Figure 2.2. Textual canvases.

based on the entire system of signs and symbols (represented in figures 2.3, 2.4, and 2.5).

At such a level of observation, it became possible to present a theory of text comprehension (Tonfoni 1989–94) and to proceed toward working out the details of an experimental environment for the development of "pure substances" in information, just as chemists can separate mixed substances using "ad hoc" filters. This is where and when and how the theory of text compression (Tonfoni 1995) was generated.

I had at this point started thinking about defining the appropriate conditions for keeping a "sterilized" environment. Based on observation of naturally occurring communicative performance, which is in fact fuzzy most of the time, meaning accretion and a certain level of "contamination" and fuzziness were expected and tolerated within the previously established setting for a theory of text comprehension. However, such fuzziness could not be tolerated

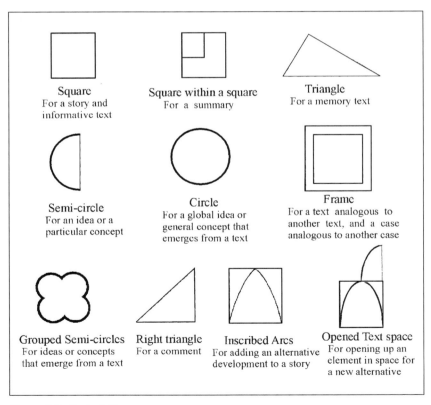

Figure 2.3. Textual Signs.

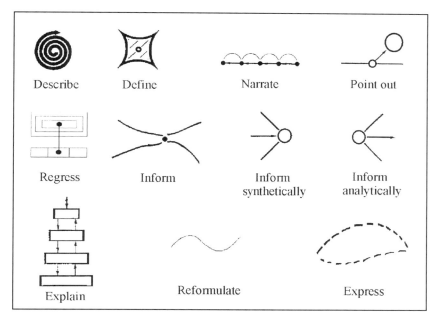

Figure 2.4. Textual symbols.

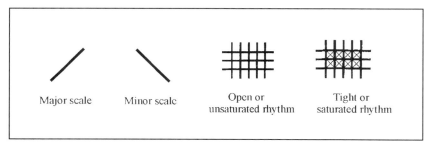

Figure 2.5. Textual turn-taking symbols.

within a framework where communication enhancement at the highest level of accuracy represents the actual target.

I then had to face the need for reinterpretation of those very same observational devices I had progressively designed and used by rethinking their respective functions at a higher degree of accuracy.

From this perspective, textual machines may be interpreted and viewed as a kind of "information distillation tool" meant to facilitate separation of different parts into their language components. These are like mixed substances, which we set and test for tolerance or boiling point just as in a "separatory tunnel." Maintaining a constant information temperature for experiments by reinterpreting textual canvases as an "incubator" resulted in a productive process. But where the power of the metaphorical environment was most effective and significant was in a sort of "Kippgenerator of textual reactions" activated by textual signs and symbols. Intermediate phases for final isolation of the pure "information substances" were also made possible through the progressive use of a "communicative desiccator" and an "information filtration device," which represented an enhanced version of the already designed "textual gridcase." This has been the experimental setting research environment I have been progressively constructing for planning, designing, and testing both theories of text comprehension and of text compression.

Metaphorical Environments

I have introduced a metaphorical environment as a conceptual dynamic structure, meant to be a reliable tool for supporting descriptions of newly defined problems and for designing ways to solve them consistently within a newly established theoretical framework. Metaphorical environments are dynamic and therefore specifically suited for expressing the complexity of the phenomenon or set of phenomena, which are meant to be represented both synthetically and analytically. It may sound contradictory and unusual to think of metaphors as analytical procedures because metaphors are conceived of and used primarily as synthetic procedures intended to establish new meaning connections. When we introduce the concept of progressive construction of a metaphorical environment, however, the possibility of introducing analytical thinking into the planning, design, and construction of articulated metaphors becomes a fact.

To better understand which important implications may be derived, let us consider the nature of a metaphor as the result of a whole process of meaning attribution and progressive redefinition. A metaphor is the result of transferring a certain meaning resulting from a selection or relevant features from one "old"—in the sense of well-established and known—domain into one "new," less established, and still vaguely designed or even almost unknown domain. The transferred meaning may be represented by a connotative or denotative element or by an entire concept or chain of concepts. Metaphors in poetry not only allow but also welcome a whole set of possible interpretations; they are therefore by definition meant to be centrifugal because they entail expression of possible meaning into different directions and paths, departing from the core definition. To assure that a scientific metaphor can adequately convey the kind of meaning intended by the researcher, it needs to undergo fundamental changes and become centripetal. This means that different kinds of meaning attribution processes will have to converge toward a very precise core definition.

A metaphor is always generated within a certain realm, which means that it comes from a certain region of meaning where different semantic attributions may occur, but only some may prevail so as to be transferred to the newly established domain. Metaphorical perception in poetry is based on such most welcome and most appropriate co-occurrence of various meanings. Scientific metaphors, however, are meant to facilitate highly specific meaning attribution in order to avoid undesired meaning accretion.

To become reliable, scientific metaphor must be conceived as part of a global framework, where the framework is a skeletal structure of meaning previously designed, set up, and checked in its own individual parts, which are interconnected and joined together. The scientific metaphor designer needs to proceed toward an accurate and highly specific definition of each of those parts to turn the "framework" into a "domain," which is a meaning territory governed by a single overall ruling principle.

Only at that point will the metaphorical domain be ready to be turned into an operative tool for articulated interpretation and understanding of a complex phenomenon or set of phenomena. In this way it becomes a metaphorical environment, within which a whole set of problems may not only be synthesized, but also analyzed and viewed from a dynamic and multidimensional perspective to be first thoroughly explained and then practically solved. To present an accurate definition of an "operationally valid metaphorical environment," we need first to analyze the process by which a metaphor proceeds from a general and well-established realm, through a carefully defined intermediate framework, and finally into a new domain for new meaning attribution.

In this process, the metaphorical structure will progressively change status, proceeding toward different stages, which may resemble those transformations occurring when an element is transferred from a "plenum" into a "vacuum" of meaning attribution.

Only after a vacuum of meaning condition has been reached may the metaphorical domain be productively turned into an operationally valid metaphorical environment. If a vacuum of meaning condition has not yet been reached, any metaphor that has not undergone a process of filtering will carry undesired contextual accretion, adding fuzziness and resulting in a misleading as opposed to a clarifying and explaining process. "Plenum of meaning" is a state or space in which an element is contained at a certain meaning attribution pressure, which is greater than the actual contextual and desired meaning attribution pressure.

The entire interpretation space has to be considered filled in with much more semantic matter than is actually needed. Much previous and undesired contextual accretion and fuzziness are present, often jeopardizing the correct and desired new contextual meaning attribution. Filtering and basic elements separation need to be activated to reduce the level of heavy contextual accretion and fuzziness.

A "vacuum of meaning" is a desirable situation to reach, for it provides an enclosed interpretation space from which contextual accretion of irrelevant semantic matter has been more or less removed. The semantic matter remaining within the interpretation space will exert less pressure than the desired contextual attribution, as opposed to what we have seen within a plenum of meaning. A vacuum of meaning represents the state of lowest semantic energy and context attribution that can ever be reached.

Visual representations of both the plenum and the vacuum of meaning for consistent design of a scientific environment appear in Figures 2.6 and 2.7. Within an appropriately and consistently constructed metaphorical environment, each of the components coming into play will be defined in its own meaning, function, and range of applications and can be interpreted consis-

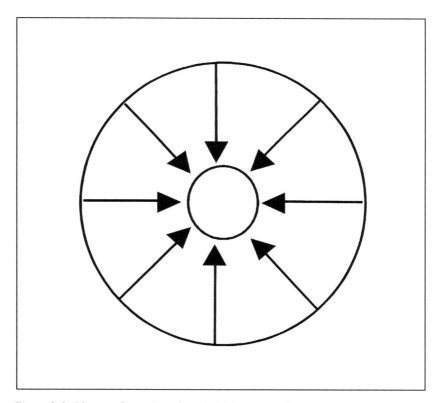

Figure 2.6. Plenum of meaning, showing high contextual pressure.

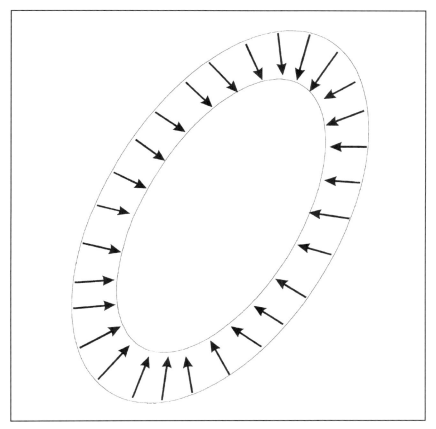

Figure 2.7. Vacuum of meaning, showing low contextual pressure.

tently and consensually. Only after an accurate definition based on rethinking and reframing will the environment be properly defined as a combination of surrounding conditions or influences for making reasoning about certain phenomena possible.

As a consequence of a shared core of precisely defined concepts, any metaphorical environment may be turned into the more comprehensive configuration of an operational model, according to which different kinds of processes are made possible. The overall configuration is based upon a precise definition of the relative disposition and arrangement of the different components. To better characterize why and how the newly defined theoretical framework may be put to work productively in order to generate consistent meaning within the field of information design, seven metaphorical environments are proposed and illustrated.

The Martial Arts for Communication Model (The MAC Model)

CPP-TRS methodology and language are based upon a set of precisely defined metaphors, textual machines, textual canvases, textual signs, textual symbols, and textual objects. The theory on which the model resides is presented in terms of a metaphorical environment, or more exactly a set of metaphorical environments aimed at accommodating different kinds of explanatory needs of natural language. An additional metaphorical environment for reframing the overall methodology is presented here.

Precisely defined metaphors as well as metaphorical environments are neither exclusive nor incompatible, if the aim is to raise the significance of a word, concept, or model that has been selected to be reframed for precise use in a new framework of reference. If carefully readapted according to different explanatory needs, it may very easily be the case that more metaphors acting synchronously and consistently as well as more metaphorical environments designed to portray the complexity of a certain realm may result in a more powerful explanatory device or set of devices altogether.

To the extent that definitions are accurately designed and relevant features indicated, a complex interaction of consistently designed metaphors may work at a higher speed and at a higher degree of precision and reliability than would just one. A certain metaphor, though accurately selected and properly redefined, may represent only some parts of a complex problem in natural language processing and information design, whereas a different metaphor may represent other parts and aspects that would otherwise be missing or just left out. Paradoxically, discontinuity is the only guarantee for continuity and completeness.

Communication is evidently such a complex realm that only a kaleidoscopic combination of different models for visualizing and expressing various aspects may result in an adequate and multilayered map reflecting and accurately modeling such inherent complexity. In this way, we may distinguish between "large scale metaphors" and "reduced scale metaphors" and between "operational metaphors" and "narrative metaphors." We can then evaluate the degree of approximation they may reach according to a set of predefined tasks. What cannot be captured by just one model may well be interpreted by the next one, still without denying the value of the previous one, which had been selected according to a set of priorities—just as a political map does not contradict a geographical map of the same area, but addresses different issues by focusing on different features.

Most important is clarity of vision and sharpness in identifying those relevant features that must first be made surface as to be consistently visualized and represented.

By proposing the martial arts framework for a better understanding of CPP-TRS methodology and language, only certain features within the definition of martial arts will be referred to, as opposed to the global meaning, which such a metaphorical environment may carry and convey in all its features. If martial arts are "systems for self-defense based on the individual's seeking and effort to attain self-mastery and enlightenment," then according to such a definition, textual communicative techniques may be consistently thought of as precise strategies for self-defense from indiscriminate information load and misunderstanding. They are in fact based on individuals' efforts to attain communicative self-awareness and mastery through progressive training. Just as in the martial arts, specific exercises are designed to promote strength once a certain and precise "cognitive weakness" has been identified. It will then be far easier to work on that to make the individual stronger, for self-awareness is the basic and fundamental condition for improvement.

Just as in karate the effectiveness of focused attacks is on weak parts, communicative techniques will apply to weak cognitive capacities by not attacking them directly, but as in aikido, by meeting the opponent's force and working with it harmoniously. Martial arts do sometime involve weapons being seen as extensions of parts of the body. The same applies to CPP-TRS, where tools are conceived as practical extensions of cognitive processes meant to amplify what the individual already has and knows and is therefore able to monitor and control. As we can see from this example, any metaphorical environment design is a twofold process: first is the determination of the user with consistent decision making about which relevant aspects among the many available need to be enlightened most; second comes the overall arrangement involving scale, symbolization, and style of concepts presentation. In this specific case entailing redefinition of an accurately and consistently reframed martial arts metaphorical environment, some highly specific aspects have been considered. In order to grasp the significance of the overall framework, some knowledge about martial arts is absolutely needed.

In contrast to literary texts and poetry, pushing metaphors beyond those limits that have been set will create possible misunderstanding. Just as mapmaking implies a surveying process with a high level of accuracy, the same level of accuracy must be applied to the planning and design of metaphorical environments. In the martial arts example, an aspect of the metaphorical environment to be explored further is *preciseness and accuracy in getting skilled in those moves which are meant to be executed in a very precise way.* Accuracy in execution is the absolute precondition for valuable performance, understanding, and preservation of the tradition itself.

A further relevant feature, which can be transferred, resides in the differentiation and ranking of different degrees of ability in the performance, ranging from a first level of exposure to the techniques up to a very high level of apprenticeship and to finally reach full expertise. The possibility of multiple ranking allows for identification of lower and higher degrees of performance within the same art.

The martial arts are based upon a combination of actions showing their own syntax, just as in CPP-TRS communicative functions and communicative intentions are not only highly compatible but also nicely combinable as they are based on some predictable pattern recognition. "Accuracy of execution" in communicative actions needs therefore to be considered as an absolutely relevant and valuable precondition, meant to create an optimal context for consistent interpretation. If we were to first focus on combinations that may be generated, as well as on those links between and among communicative functions that show precisely in text in textual signs, we may certainly see that some links are much stronger and much more predictable than others. We may then also recognize more potentially active links that may be activated from communicative function combinations and are affecting communicative intention represented by textual symbols. Thus signs may open up expectations about very specific symbols, which implies that the global communicative function of a text may trigger some stronger expectations about local communicative intentions, just as some combination and coordination of movements are more likely to appear than another in the actual performance of martial arts.

After global communicative function has been made explicit, there are other kinds of strong links that are active at the local level of communicative intention expectations in a sequence. Combinations of various communicative moves have to be interpreted as harmoniously progressing and nicely evolving sequences of actions in time. At this point, the combination of communicative moves will resemble dance moves alternating through accurate indication of rhythm. Here the original metaphor will have to shift context, progressively entering the realm of music and musical notation, which is one of the first metaphorical environments I proposed for the interpretation of the communicative notation system. Shifting contexts for harmonious interpretation is a fundamental condition for accurate interpretation and consistent bridging of those gaps that would not possibly be filled and adequately handled within the same metaphor.

Another observation, which derives from the martial arts realm and metaphorical framework, is related to the kind of teaching and learning processes that martial arts entail. If we think of teaching as a way to open up possible paths for further development, the teacher is there to assist the learner periodically, so that the learner can move autonomously into multiple directions, with some kind of centrifugal motion in learning. This is certainly not the kind of teaching and learning suitable for martial arts. In the martial arts, techniques transmission is one of the most crucial points for the learner, who must reproduce at the highest level of accuracy a certain set of moves. Accurate observation of the teacher, imitation of observed behavior, repetition, and refinement are the progressively evolving stages of a process meant for the learner to reach the highest possible degree of approximation of an idealized and preset behavior. Teaching within well defined constraints is therefore mostly training and by definition centripetal, which means that it originates from the teacher and the learner is stimulated to emulate the teacher, by pushing the model to the highest possible degree of approximation up to "perfection." Conservation of the tradition of martial arts is based upon preservation of precisely defined skills and cautiously acquired knowledge. Learning a system of communication based on moves and skills acquisition is therefore primarily based on a centripetal move of teaching, very much like the one of the martial arts.

Preservation of a "certain art of doing things" means having actions happen through progressive approximation toward an idealized state of performance. Modification of currently transmitted patterns is therefore viewed as something that may diminish the value of those very same patterns that are meant to be preserved. Any martial art may be therefore considered to be a stabilized system to be kept and preserved as such. Different degrees of quality in performance have to be related to the level of apprenticeship and progressive knowledge disclosure. Teaching conceived as a process of accurate skills transmission may also be found in the teaching of dancing and music. In coordinating dancing by a single dancer and within groups, aspects such as precision in time and spatial movement configuration are fundamental. It is obvious that no group of dancers could ever be coordinated by a single dance director if centripetal learning mechanisms were not active. By combining more metaphorical environments to specify a certain concept, it becomes evident that apparent discontinuity in shifting from one realm into another may actually represent the unique and fundamental condition for continuity in full meaning rendering and overall reconfiguration. Accurate planning and designing of each metaphor and metaphorical environment will therefore result in a process that must be made explicit in all its details in order to create the basic conditions for precise explanation and full visibility of the newly established framework.

The Architecture and Arch Model (The ARCH Model)

All of my work on language and information is based on the fundamental assumptions that a text may be conceived, designed, planned, and organized as a building and that more accurate planning will result in a better and more functional construction. The metaphorical environment presented here is based on a single word, "arch," which triggers two different semantic domains, two metaphorical environments, which may harmoniously coexist. They are "architecture" and "arch."

Let us begin by analyzing the first semantic domain, triggered by "architecture," in more detail. The architectural model is a metaphor opening up the possibility of viewing text as a complex architectural structure and as a whole new way of conceiving language and information organization as text planning, designing, and architecturing. "Architecture" is defined in the Random House dictionary as "the profession of designing buildings, open areas and other artificial constructions and environments, usually with some regard to aesthetic effect. Architecture often includes design or selection of furnishings and decorations, supervision of construction work and the examination, restoration or remodeling of existing buildings."

Textual architecture covers a whole set of different activities, ranging from the design of highly functionalized texts to the definition of open spaces for communication flows. It also includes the design of precisely built-in artificial text constructions, covering text decoration as well as text restoration and remodeling. I have defined those terms in both their theoretical and practical implications to make sure they represent and convey effectively and unambiguously the kind of operations that need to be described and defined in the process of text construction, conceived both in terms of an individually planned and a collectively performed enterprise. Reframing such concepts will lead to a better and more effective way of interpreting operations that are very distinct but, if not observed and carefully defined, may appear fuzzy and mixed. Recognizing them as both synchronously and asynchronously active is an extremely valuable procedure for creating consensus and context for accurate interpretation and definition of what performance in language really is.

Just as architects plan and design as a fundamental precondition for activating and monitoring the construction of the actual building and just as they share a terminology to talk about and supervise the actual construction, I have specifically identified some very precise terminology to be used to name operations having been performed, being performed, or to be performed upon text, both synchronously and asynchronously.

The fact that architecture is both art and science is also an extremely relevant feature of the metaphorical environment to be extended to the art and science of text construction. While in architecture there are precise laws to be respected and constraints to be referred to that are related to the kind of material to be used, personal styles may be developed and openly recognized. The same happens in the construction of texts built with different languages and through different and personal styles. They all reside on strongly grounded and fundamental principles of communication and laws of cognitive balance in order to be accepted, placed in context, and recognized as functional according to a predefined function or set of functions to be exploited. Reframing the overall organization of a text in terms of accurate balance between laws of construction and possibilities of variation correctly reflects the complexity of the task itself.

The architect also needs to be seen as a scientist who is fully aware of the physical laws that rule construction and of the chemical properties of the material that will be used. The architect is a skilled technician, as well, able to adapt expertise to the task or set of tasks, and an artist able to approximate through planning and design the ideal construction model. Tension between reality based upon objective constraints and idealized models to then be implemented represents the fundamental condition for any further stage of evolution in the planning of any construction. This is one reason I have pushed the architectural metaphorical environment so far. I am then able to think and predict the possibility of environmentally sound textual buildings to be harmoniously integrated within an already existing context of communication or structuring of compressed material for accelerating the building process under specific circumstances and for very precise functions.

From the same metaphorical environment other possible links may be productively established between and among properties of specific communication material being used. This allows for the possibility of appropriate evaluation of easiness or lightness and the insulation or resistance of a certain communicative construction having first been conceived and then built. Pressure of information and thickness and pressure on the communicative construction may be made subject to evaluation according to redefined and preset parameters. It can be carefully quantified, therefore allowing for enhancement in communicative performance, based on consistently set criteria and high visibility of evaluation parameters. Evaluation of language in this way was not possible prior to Chomsky's (1957) work on syntactic correctness.

Within the textlinguistics framework (De Beaugrande and Dressler 1981), seven basic conditions for textuality were set which have proved applicable to more analytical descriptions of text understanding. By introducing the concept of "text perception" as opposed to text reception or understanding, I wanted to explicitly and precisely refer to the existence of multiple layers and different dimensions of understanding in text processing. The need to identify and separately handle these layers and dimensions underlines once again the fundamental role research in knowledge representation has played in enlightening and capturing new levels of description through the introduction of dynamic representation systems such as the frame (Minsky 1975), the script (Schank 1980), the plan (Wilensky 1983), and the plot unit (Lehnert 1981). By extending the realm of application of the concept of text perception, the relevance of precise decision making by the text designer is stressed, particularly in reference to typology, functionality, and style of the communicative construction to be perceived, used, and comfortably "inhabited" by its respective users. Terms such as "text rotation" have therefore become fundamental tools for operating text based on a precise definition of their operational and practical meaning.

Let us now proceed toward an accurate description of the metaphorical environment triggered by the word "arch" applied to its second semantic domain—that is, the concept and object "arch." "Arch" is defined in the Random House dictionary as "a curved masonry construction for spanning an opening consisting of a number of wedgelike stones, bricks or the like, set with the narrower side toward the opening in such a way that forces on the arch are transmitted as vertical or obliques stresses on either side of the opening." Though arches may vary according to their style, they do share a precise set of properties (Winston 1982). To allow for the existence of an arch, it is essential to plan for a set of links and harmonious relationships among different kinds of material and forces active upon the overall structure. Material chosen may be of different kinds and show very specific characteristics; iron, wood, and brick, by comparison, share some commonalities, but also show a whole set of different properties. The same applies to the variety of languages, which may share basic structures but show a whole set of differences, both at the syntactic and the semantic levels. Material therefore means, within the metaphorical environment now illustrated, the specific language being used.

Those forces applied to an arch are precisely the "pulling apart tension" and the "pushing together compression." A skilled observer may easily identify the interplay of those forces in the overall construction as a harmoniously evolving process of alternation and structures, just as a building reflects the harmonious interplay of tension and compression working together. In the structure of an arch, compression applies to the upper part, which is the vertex of the arch itself, whereas tension works at the bottom and at both lateral parts.

I have reframed the concept of "arch" to create a metaphorical environment for sound interpretation for theories both of text comprehension (Tonfoni 1989–94) and of text compression (Tonfoni 1995). These are meant to create the structure for thinking and operating on language at different levels of complexity but with a commonly shared terminology and a consistently organized set of tools. To better visualize the intrinsic relationship between those theories in their mutual interplay, more global rethinking and reframing of the arch concept are needed. (See figure 2.8.)

Within the theory of text comprehension, I have focused primarily on the high level of complexity that is evident in interactions occurring through natural language, whereas complexity will necessarily cause tension within the theory of text compression. I have proceeded toward enhancing some specific aspects of communication occurring through natural language, therefore producing compression effects upon different kinds of texts. To keep an arch in equilibrium, a good balance between tension and compression is needed. The same principle applies to an arch framework for thinking and reframing of natural language phenomena. A mutual interplay of those forces is needed as to create an adequately balanced status for the arch itself.

To keep an actual arch together, different components are needed, all of which have to be combinable, compatible, and linked together to provide equilibrium to the overall structure. The same applies to a global framework for a theory of language, consisting of different and distinct components, all of which are meant to support each other. Within the arch metaphorical frame-

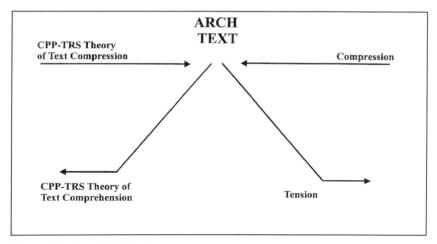

Figure 2.8. The ARCH Model 1.

work, the keystone is that specific element that keeps the arch together but varies according to different priorities set at different times. To better visualize the arch-balanced system for language processing, an actual arch may serve as an adequate model to then be transferred to the distinctive components of a more general framework for interpreting language and a very wide range of specific phenomena occurring via natural language. To properly represent the coordination of different components within an arch, the model must be viewed dynamically, which means that equilibrium must be viewed as a complex interplay among different components. (See figure 2.9.)

Handling just one aspect of communication via natural language will therefore imply prioritizing a certain component first and focusing on it without forgetting about the strong influence other components have and the specific role of support they play. Specificity and interconnectivity result in two compatible aspects within the overall metaphorical environment for describing, defining, and explaining communication phenomena in natural language. Textual canvases have been designed and used as a kind of "textual microscope" meant to enlighten very precise phenomena occurring in text and then proceed toward the designing and applying of a "textual gridcase" based on the entire system of textual signs and textual symbols.

The Union Station Indoor Model (The USI Model)

A complex system with flows of information coming from different directions and performing different functions undergoes a whole set of changes and transformations that need to be represented accurately. Any metaphorical

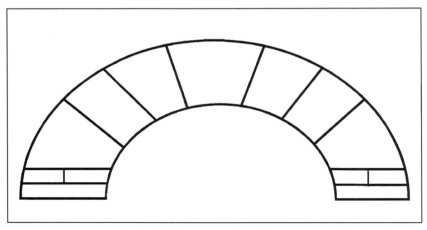

Figure 2.9. The ARCH Model 2.

environment meant to capture and interpret such complexity must result in a highly articulated system. It must also allow for multiple layers of interpretation and processing. To effectively represent such a complex mechanism with qualitatively different flows of information coming in, which then must be converted into precisely functionalized texts, I have chosen the carefully observed environment of Union Station in Washington, D.C.

As I previously noted, the final output structure will show some features of the originating structure, but will not reflect the overall originating structure, which will undergo a set of reinterpretation processes. What is kept is the core of the relevant features.

To clarify the concept of transferring some relevant features from a physical to a metaphorical environment, let me give a brief example from impressionist painting. While painting a party on a boat with his friends in conversation, Jean Renoir was actually grasping "flashes" from the scene, but those flashes represented what was most relevant about the personalities of his friends. The same point could be made about Toulouse-Lautrec, who tried to fix on canvas the dynamics of movement and dancing while observing it. Features he selected for representation were those that conveyed precisely the recognizable personality traits of the individuals being portrayed. What may look like "impressions" is in fact the result of a careful process of selecting relevant features. Without such accurate selection by the painter, observers of the painting would not be able to identify those individuals, personalities, and emotions that are so vividly portrayed.

The same principle applies to the selection of relevant features in a highly articulated environment meant to be viewed both statically and dynamically in order to grasp and represent aspects of communication. The USI Model is a three-layered model for information-processing, in which three different floors represent different kinds of operations being performed upon information coming in. The top level, the first floor, is characterized by a highly continuous and dishomogeneous flow of information, which is still unprocessed and comes from different directions. The information coming in the form of different texts and showing different degrees of complexity is also very fuzzy and must be filtered and organized before it can be accessed and used. The model of information flow and text recollection on the first floor is centripetal. This means that incoming information must undergo a process of filtering and restructuring, performed by a team of skilled operators who make decisions about which level of preprocessing or prepackaging should be used for each text or sequence of texts at any given time.

Once the selection has been made, texts will be moved to the second floor to be processed and stored according to the theory of text comprehension (Tonfoni 1989–94). They will be indexed, catalogued, and labelled according to their communicative positioning by undergoing an interpretation process that does not affect the nature of each text. By carrying a set of indications about their functionality, texts will be much easier to process and more easily identified for access according to different users' needs. Content distribution will largely reflect the originating structure, and no major changes have occurred because a shallow filtering process has been used.

To substantially increase the quality of texts and the visibility of the content, in-depth text reprocessing will be needed. In this process, preprocessed texts coming from the second level proceed toward a third level of compression represented by the third floor. Those texts, which have been reorganized according to the theory of text comprehension, will undergo a further reconfiguration at a higher level of accuracy according to the theory of text compression. At the third floor, text compression and high speed and acceleration in text are made possible. This movement from first floor to second floor to third floor reflects a progressive "in-depth search" in the model. If users can access information actively on the second floor, they will also be able to access information at a higher speed and within the optimized environment of the third floor.

High concentration and high density should be the most relevant features of highly sophisticated knowledge reconfiguration processes and readjustment, and should result into an optimized environment. Determining the kinds of texts to be found at the second floor as opposed to those reconfigured for the third floor is the text operators' crew decision. At the first floor, this crew decides on the level of processing each text should undergo.

There is a clearly evident qualitative difference between a preliminary preprocessing stage leading toward the configuration of an integrated environment, such as the one located on the second floor, and an empowered high speed and high compression informative environment such as the one located on the third floor. Users approaching information organized in highly compressed textual units at the third floor will gain specific insight very quickly and directly about very specific topics within well defined areas of knowledge. If the first floor is organized according to a centripetal model of textual information-gathering, coordinating, and packaging, and the second floor is based on a multiple direction organization for information-seeking and navigation, then the third floor is based on a highly sophisticated textual cartography meant to easily direct users to quickly access and process information to enable them to return to their own tasks after fulfilling their needs. The third floor reflects therefore a centrifugal model for textual knowledge access and further use. (The USI Model is represented in figure 2.10.)

Users accessing both the second and third floors may be viewed as different

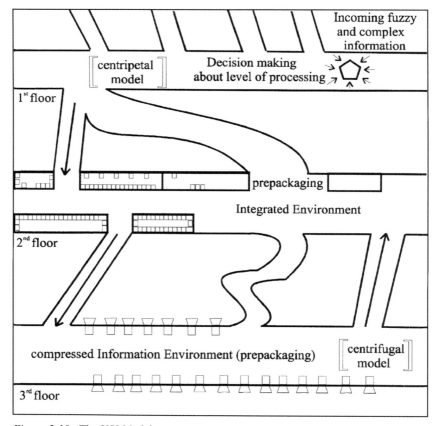

Figure 2.10. The USI Model.

individuals accessing the building for different reasons, but they may also be the same individuals experiencing two quantitatively and qualitatively different ways of seeking textual information. An important thing for them to know is how these two approaches differ and to what extent knowledge reconfiguration is different according to the degree of accuracy. For this reason, a diversified definition for theories of text comprehension and compression respectively is needed. The goal is to distinguish a more approximate stage of text processing represented by the concept of "comprehension" from a precisely defined and accurately specified stage of text processing represented by the concept of "compression." This is also why distinguishing between complementary aspects of the same system is productive, leading as it does toward the need for two distinct though highly complementary theories.

The Union Station Outdoor Model (The USO Model)

A complex system such as natural language requires accurate decision making about which kind of textual information should undergo which kind of processing. It is therefore useful to think in terms of different levels of density for the same kind of material (represented by natural language organized into texts) and in terms of organic versus inorganic substances (represented by different codes). The Union Station Outdoor Model supports accurate rethinking about differently processed textual information units because it represents fundamental differences in the levels of granularity and the kinds of concrete units used and combined. Some areas show the combination of enlarged structures, whereas others are characterized by highly reduced structures in the overall planning of pavement. (This variety is represented in figure 2.11.)

To better specify the concept visualized in the USO model, we should first note that some information areas have been processed and reconfigured according to the theory of text comprehension (Tonfoni 1989–94) at a lower degree of textual preprocessing, whereas some other information areas are characterized by a higher degree of textual preprocessing according to the theory of text compression (Tonfoni 1995).

It becomes increasingly evident that accurate decision making about the kind of preprocessing to be activated on which kind of textual information is a most fundamental issue. While some information territories may allow for some fuzziness, some others require full clarity and transparency, therefore posing the need to apply the same system at full speed and with full power. The same "CPP-TRS logics" works as an engine to be applied to texts at different levels of intensity and speed and is to be carefully monitored. It also becomes relevant to consider whether such an engine is being used or will be used just as an interpreter or as a generator for preprocessing texts. It then must be clearly defined as to how much power and at which speed this will

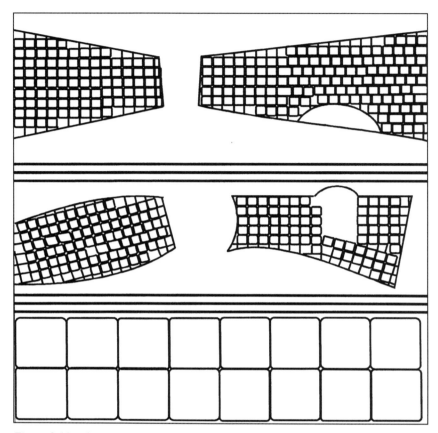

Figure 2.11. The USO Model 1.

happen. Here is where the most important process of decision making comes into play.

Strong assumptions within this operational model are that any communication flow must be checked, monitored, and controlled by communicative partners within the communication context, because natural language is in itself a very unstable and quite unreliable system if not properly monitored, controlled, and consistently processed. For this reason, revision stages and multiple operations on incoming textual information are both needed and welcome in order to enhance the quality of the overall performance. Such revision stages are the result of optimization procedures, which may be expensive if fully exploited and therefore need to be carefully planned. CPP-TRS may be used as an engine to enhance text understanding at different degrees of intensity. Some balance is required as the entire information texture may not be optimized and different degrees of enhancement may need to be planned. Not all of the information texture is eligible for optimization processes, so wide areas may be left the way they are or they may undergo a limited set of pre-processing operations mainly addressed toward enhancing preidentified knowledge areas.

At this point it is once more useful to refer to the architectural metaphorical environment because architecture is not only the science of construction but also the science of leaving open spaces unbuilt to fit a more global view of territorial planning. This is like language, where a harmoniously organized combination of utterances and silence creates meaning.

The concept of "granularity" has been applied with great success to knowledge organization and processing (Hobbs 1985) according to both theories of text comprehension (Tonfoni 1989–94) and compression (Tonfoni 1995). If knowledge is subject to the constraints of granularity, it is quite natural that such a condition will reflect upon information conveyed via natural language. Given the massive quantity of information flows, it makes more and more sense to think in terms of different stages of information processing, as well as different levels of availability and access to knowledge, according to a set of prestated and predefined information needs. Textual information to be processed at qualitatively different levels of accuracy and density will be embedded and incorporated within a certain information territory. This will then be organized according to its topical consistency and continuity. Purified textual information will have to be contextualized appropriately to fulfill the primary conditions in order to be interpreted consistently. Time and space shifts are potential obstacles for appropriate interpretation and understanding. This is why a fundamental distinction between "organic" and "inorganic" textual matter is needed to explicitly recognize the possibility of upgrading the communicative value of each inorganic textual unit by complementing it with the appropriate context to ensure accurate interpretation through time and space shifts. Since new terms and definitions are a fundamental tool for a better and deeper understanding and interpretation of a new framework, the concept of CPTRU (Communicatively Positioned Textually Represented Unit), which means context-recreated-text, is of direct use to ensure that information conveyed in the form of texts may be appropriately processed and recognized through space and time without any loss or shift in the original definition.

The USO Model is meant to represent various density levels in textual information, which has been processed together with its originating "context," to fit within a certain wider information territory and to be recognized and processed according to its most appropriate meaning. Textual information is spread around a wide territory, so users will have to search for what they are really looking for and will have to be assisted by visual information elements representing the overall organization. Figure 2.12 shows the overall configu-

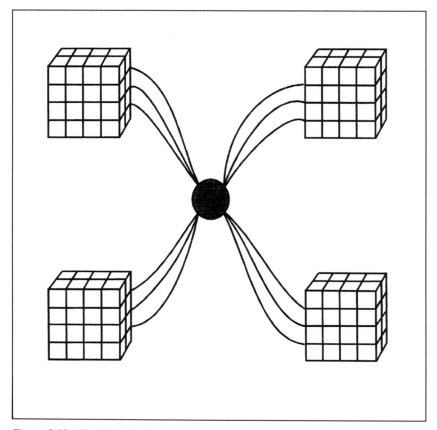

Figure 2.12. The USO Model 2.

ration of organized information territory made of context at different degrees of accuracy and density.

In this way users will become aware of the "information quality" of each textual information unit, which will be accessed and recognized in its functionality, structure, and density. According to the USI Model, different levels of access to information are possible as a result of a highly differentiated model of prepackaging textual units represented by the different floors. This process operates in the same way; users accessing the USO Model will be able to "see" and be informed about the qualitative preprocessing operations that have been activated upon different textual units according to different kinds of pavement configuration. Different "information islands" within the same territory indicate the different kind of information being organized.

The USI and USO models are therefore complementary models and must be conceived of as continuous as well. The decision-making process activated to organize knowledge will refer back to the same set of architectural principles, harmoniously linking together open spaces and buildings. Neither the USI nor the USO model works under stabilized conditions, for indoor and outdoor conditions such as light and temperature change all the time. Both USI and USO models show information that is still exposed to a variety of changes and external interferences, though insulated and resistant.

To explore different possibilities raised by a stabilized environment, a new metaphorical environment is needed.

The Pentagon City Mall Model (The PCM Model)

When I first planned to design a further metaphorical framework based on a highly articulated model such as the Pentagon City Mall, I intended to represent the possibility of accurately organizing already compressed textual information within a stabilized environment. Compressed textual information is most useful when fast and effective access to information is needed and speed is as important as accuracy. If not appropriately processed, textual information is subject to misinterpretation and different kinds of deformation, especially when a textual unit is transitioning from a certain context to another. Once a set of textual units has been found to be particularly relevant to organize and access rapidly, then the need for a most appropriate textual building arises.

The Pentagon City Mall Model is characterized by stabilized conditions: temperature is stable as well as light, which means that, within the metaphorical environment, information building is insulated in such a way that communication pressure does not interfere with information temperature in any way. The context has been stabilized and made uniform to favor homogeneous access and accurate processing. To assure that temperature is stabilized and textual information coming from the outside is consistently processed and highly regulated, no indiscriminate and unregulated flow of information is ever allowed, and entrance of preprocessed textual information is strictly controlled to ensure an adequate level for those textual units stored within the same building. The PCM Model is therefore an "ad hoc" representation of accurate storage of textual information in a "continuum" of interpretation. No interruption is either planned or foreseen once the process has been initiated. No external interferences have to be expected.

Continuity of context constitutes a tremendously powerful aspect for facilitating knowledge absorption and compression of textual information. This represents quite an expensive process in terms of resources, time, and effort needed. Accurate decision making about the kind of textual information to be compressed and stored needs therefore to be planned in order to proceed toward appropriate information territories definition and consistent topical search. Many textual revision states will be necessary before coming up with an overall problem resolution strategy.

Compression of textual information within the PCM Model also implies a high degree of acceleration in text perception and consistent and accurate processing. In other words, not only access to "cleared" textual information is made available, but highly consistent integration of textual information within the same building is made possible. The need to recognize particularly strong links between and among textual units, some of which are more predictable and expected than others, has been analyzed and demonstrated in Tonfoni (1996).

The PCM Model is based upon a highly complex configuration designed according to a precisely defined set of predictability links, which have first been identified to result in a harmonious configuration of textual units' territories. Any textual information-seeking process is therefore accelerated and optimized. A carefully designed composition of the overall textual information-building and structure implies that the visitor has initiated a certain kind of information search without trying to disconnect it. Once activated, the mechanism will proceed in a precise way and toward a precise direction according to a certain path.

If the search is initiated for analytical purposes, specific textual units will be searched "in depth," whereas a search initiated for synthetic purposes will create the need for different kinds of textual units to come into play. Just as an elevator programmed to go all the way up must complete the path in that direction first before going down, and any request to interrupt the process mid-course will be both inappropriate and ineffective, the same will happen with any textual information search process based on moving up and down carefully organized territories of compact and consistently linked textual information units. The overall PCM Model shows in its articulated structure in figure 2.13.

To fully understand the concept of the compressed text unit, it is important to refer back to the overall model and framework of information, where both text producer and text perceiver are viewed as protagonists acting together to reduce the bandwidth and distance of each text by operating consensually in order to reduce fuzziness occurring in communication via natural language. Keeping control over the context is by itself a guarantee of distance reduction through a set of consensually monitored operations upon the interpretive level, after fuzziness has first been reduced significantly or eliminated. Stabilization of conditions for interpretation plays a crucial role in understanding text. This guarantees that textual information gets processed and transferred consistently from one context into a different one without losing any important part of it. The PCM Model is, by definition, a conservative model designed to fulfill the needs for keeping special textual information in control and under stabilized conditions.

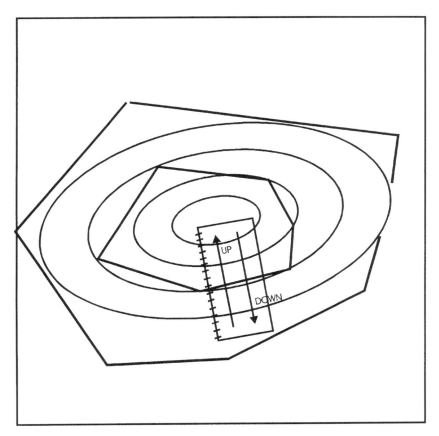

Figure 2.13. The PCM Model.

Highly specialized and no disclosure textual information will be organized to make effective searches possible. Special conditions meant to avoid disturbance, distortion, or interference, which may produce a whole set of wrong inferencing processes, will also be met. How is continuity of a topic kept within a model based upon some directionality principle? It is guaranteed by the very same predictability links that have been established among textual units. The overall configuration results in a very accurate design involving layers and levels of information distributed and coordinated to facilitate use by visitors.

The user may be viewed as a visitor accessing a new place, through a visit within a large and articulated environment with just a few moments of actual access to accelerated and compressed textual units. Once textual information has been processed, compressed, and accelerated, it is absolutely relevant to check and monitor times of exposure to such qualitatively different, because artificially recreated, matter. Just as a substantial difference exists between absorbing vitamins from oranges or pressed oranges and even more between oranges and vitamin C pills, a comparable difference exists at different levels of processing qualitatively different kinds of information.

Access to differently organized textual units at a reduced interpretation bandwidth needs to be controlled. Any stabilized context should be accurately explored and monitored so that possible collateral effects are not produced, just as some medicines may produce an undesirable outcome in patients if not monitored. Highly compressed environments therefore not only need clearance of information, but also require accurate identification of each individual visitor's needs, according to each individual "portability" and cognitive profile.

Indiscriminate access to compressed and highly accelerated textual units may result in a problem for those individuals who have been exposed to such a "very special environment" without having been made aware of its special features and properties. The potential of an information building such as the one represented in the PCM Model may be easily compared to the potential of a "powerplant." Its structure is in fact ready for further deep processes of transformation to occur and very radically impact the overall structure itself. I am referring to the activation of deep kernel processes as radiation, which may occur and be performed upon a preset structure such as the one represented by the PCM Model.

Transitions among the different though complementary models are made possible through a switchboard—a structural command unit on which are mounted switches and instruments necessary to activate different kinds of radiation on different parts of the previously defined and described model. A lightboard, a panel of switches for controlling the radiation lighting at different levels and throughout different layers of information, is also needed.

The Subway Surfacing Information-Seeking Model (The SSIS Model)

The Subway Surfacing Information-Seeking Model (SSIS Model) represents dynamic information-seeking under expert guidance. Expectations about which kind of information and where it is likely to be found are generated by a sound representation based upon a preliminary but accurate definition of information territories. It is first important to explain that the kind of textual information discussed here is subject to the same conditions that are relevant to the theory of text comprehension (Tonfoni 1989–94), but not to the conditions that are part of the theory of text compression (Tonfoni 1995).

Texts have been organized and processed so as to be better "comprehended" and have been appropriately and consistently annotated to enhance understanding and visibility of information. The SSIS Model is meant to represent a new metaphorical environment for facilitating mapping of enhanced quality and visibility of information in texts. In other words, what the SSIS Model shows is a variety of different paths for accessing knowledge conveyed textually, after appropriate text-processing has occurred to make knowledge more transparent. The SSIS Model represents an enhanced dynamic network for accessing information territories quickly and accurately at the same time. Not only does the new metaphorical framework entail the actual subway, it also entails other means of transportation at the surface level. Different means of transportation will represent and reflect different knowledge needs and modes of access to information.

In order to access the information subway, users will be requested to define their information needs accurately, just as a passenger will have to think of the destination to make sure to get on the right train and perhaps transfer to a bus. No access is feasible before the location and priorities for reaching it have been determined. Because there are different possibilities available to reach the same location, important factors such as time, number of train changes, and bus transfers should be very carefully analyzed before making any kind of final decision. Accurate definition of knowledge needs is a fundamental precondition for consistent information seeking. Guidance will only be supported once knowledge needs have been defined and modes of access prioritized consistently.

The SSIS Model underlines the responsibility each individual has and promotes active personal choices. Multiple options are particularly important as they facilitate responsible attitudes. Once a choice has been made about the information territory to be accessed together with an appropriate combination of different but compatible transportation means, it will then become particularly significant to think about timing. Time spent to decide which kind of access to a textual information territory should be chosen differs from time spent for actual navigation of textual information territories in a fundamental way. Accurate planning on both sides is required to guarantee a successful search.

Other aspects should be considered highly relevant, as they are related to motivations leading the user through a textual information search process. The user may have to first reach and then search a certain textual information territory in order to capture and absorb knowledge as part of a learning process; or the user may just browse for some fast information not necessarily meant to be retained, although the information does need to be made handy for future use. Because there is a fundamental difference between those distinctive attitudes, time for information-seeking will radically differ according to the choice of "in-depth" or "in-breadth" search. All of these aspects have to be carefully considered and planned before initiating the search process. This does not mean that a certain choice may not be changed. Any metaphorical environment is by nature dynamically organized, and special attention should be paid to revision or further planning that may occur in the course of the process.

Each subway exit represents the entrance to a certain information territory. As soon as visitors surface, they will find a high consistency and coherence of topic-related information and will not have to bounce around. Higher consistency of texts organized around each topic will be ensured by visual cues directing visitors toward those locations specifically related to information needs. The overall territory is encoded and preorganized in different regions according to preplanned paths, which are stable and reflect predictability links among textual signs and symbols. These represent communicative functions and communicative intentions according to the theory of text comprehension (Tonfoni 1989–94). To reach various kinds of information, multiple means of transportation are provided to show the fundamental distinctions among different styles of searching, different purposes, and different criteria. Different transportation modes also entail different times for knowledge absorption.

Navigation is driven by a consistent choice made earlier and is facilitated by a highly articulated system for information traffic control. Specific directions about other possible topics, which may be useful and strictly related to the originally searched topic, are provided at each information subway exit. These facilitate access by informing each visitor about directions, locations, and correspondencies among different locations. There is a need to underline the fact that information territories surrounding information subway stops are bound to lower resolution text processing, which means that those texts presented are complemented by the notation system at a rather shallow level and that the overall textual configuration is not deeply affected as would be the case if texts had undergone a further process of compression. Nevertheless visualization of information components becomes a tremendously powerful way for facilitating navigation and interpretation around wide information areas and for connecting topics, which may be productively linked together to facilitate the process of understanding. A representation of an encoded territory ready to be navigated according to the SSIS Model is shown in figure 2.14.

Just like a city subway system, differently encoded territories are closely related and connected to facilitate navigation from one territory to another one. High density of information as well as spread-out information territories require application of the SSIS Model to ensure accurate navigation and to facilitate coordination among individuals who need to access and share knowledge cooperatively.

The Communicative Ecosystem and Envelope Language Model (The CEEL Model)

I started thinking about communication as based on a variety of different languages and different codes which altogether constitute an "ecosystem."

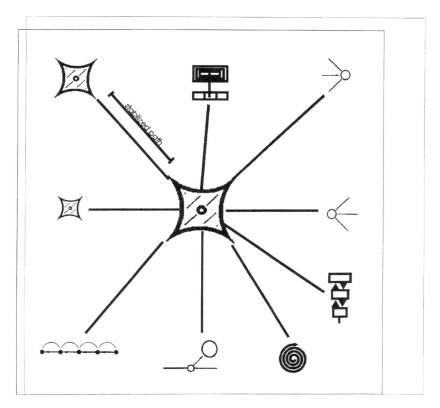

Figure 2.14. The SSIS Model.

Such a term may be applied to the "cognitive profile" of each individual communicating and acting within a wider organization, in terms of "micro-ecosystem" and to the organization itself in terms of "macroecosystem." Consistent with such distinctions, the basic need for harmonious balance among different cognitive capabilities is of crucial relevance.

Such concepts may easily be extended to everyday life communication systems working together. In the next context, an ecosystem represents a new metaphorical environment, which is in place prior to the building of a metaphorical environment. Each model presented here is meant to visualize and explain highly specific aspects within the more complex framework of information envisioned as a kind of matter showing in different states. The concept of communicative ecosystem comes before any building and architecturing model and refers to the many and different languages and codes working together and "inhabiting" the same environment.

A communicative ecosystem is therefore meant to take into account languages at any level. It is by nature a complex, interactive, and dynamically organized setting and, like other complex systems, it shows some very precise properties. A communicative ecosystem is more precisely characterized by the following set of properties:

- it has and shows interactive components and parts;
- it uses some energy, which produces wastes;
- it may be subject to malfunction; and
- it may be influenced by other systems at different degrees.

In nature, ecosystems appear as dynamic communities of organisms interacting with each other and their environment. In communication, ecosystems appear as dynamic clusters of languages interrelated and interacting with each other in their respective communicative environment. As in nature, a communicative ecosystem may be based on living and nonliving parts, where living biological parts, in this case natural languages, interact with nonliving parts, which may be represented by inorganic languages. They have been introduced in this way through the theory of text compression (Tonfoni 1995), and they interact with each other according to the theory of text comprehension (Tonfoni 1989–94). It is a fact that nonliving, chemical, and physical parts make up the ecosystem's environment, just as "physically and chemically" conceived language elements reinforce the communicative ecosystem's environment. These need to be well balanced, and such balance needs to be retained.

A communicative ecosystem may be subject to very disruptive factors, which may undermine and even destroy it completely. Those negative elements may be defined as "stress factors" and may be categorized according to the degrees of power they are likely to show. The main disruptive stress factors for a communicative ecosystem are the following:

- excess of unruled information overflowing, causing information unbalanced overgrowth;
- topical erosion caused by communication gaps and information leaks;
- underseeking or overseeking of information leading toward cognitive disturbance by individuals living within an unbalanced communicative ecosystem; and
- information distortion and information workload storms leading to communication dysfunctions and chronic diseases due to persistence of cognitively unhealthy and unbalanced conditions for individuals inhabiting the same communicative ecosystem.

A communicative ecosystem may produce and use energy and, at the same time, may also produce information waste. Recycling therefore becomes a substantial need, actually representing an important way to manage information effectively by reprocessing and reusing it for different purposes.

Information intended to undergo a recycling process needs first to be accurately collected. This implies an accurate decision making process. It is then sorted and reprocessed in order to create new informative material. Any recycling process is meant to encourage use of information wastes to generate new communication energy. In other words it may happen that information, which may decay within a certain environment, becomes transportable after accurate sorting and reprocessing within a different environment. Such an event is possible through consistent definition of transitional stages in processing information and in planning on transformations, which may take place in the form of textual revision states.

Let us now more carefully specify the concept of communicative ecosystem, which is a system formed through interaction of many and various languages within a certain information environment and includes the aggregate of surrounding conditions and influences related to a specific knowledge domain. Within a communicative ecosystem, languages may be viewed as organisms. The meaning attributed by the Random House dictionary to the term "organism" is "any complex thing or system having properties and functions determined not only by the properties and relations of its individual parts, but by the character of the whole that they compose and by the relations of the parts to the whole."

Individuals need to be able to communicate with each other through the use of different languages and codes. This is why the concept of "envelope language" (EL) may be very useful, and the CPP-TRS methodology and language may be presented as a very effective envelope language. An envelope is a container in the specific sense of a surrounding or enclosing structure, where combinations of icons will serve to inform receivers about the communicative structure of each information package coming in at a given time. Just as an envelope may contain different kinds of messages and be made with different kinds of paper, an envelope language like CPP-TRS may apply to different languages including visual ones.

An envelope language is therefore a metaphorical envelope complementing another system of communication, which will convey precisely what the other system of communication does not convey but from which it could benefit. It may more rapidly convey the communicative function of a text through the communicative intention and the communicative turn by going paragraph by paragraph and sentence by sentence. Stamped on each single metaphorical message envelope will be the most appropriate combination for indicating the communicative value of each. Additional information about the specific kind of text preprocessing activated upon each single text allowing for more or less effective delivery will also be indicated.

It becomes quite evident that different levels of processing applied to texts according to the same principle will open up the possibility of an accurate evaluation and ranking process, addressing frequency in ordering different strings of information coming in as well as intensity of knowledge conveyed by each textual unit. Measuring is made possible through the Textually Organized Notation Frequency for Ordering Navigation Intensity (TONFONI) parameters and conditions. "Frequency" here means the rate of occurrence at which the CPP-TRS-based enhancing mechanism has been applied to incoming textual strings. "Intensity" means the quality or condition of being intense, where intense applied to a certain text unit indicates that such unit is effective and is easily transportable because of the high communicative energy being developed. An enhancing mechanism is meant to both intensify and magnify a certain effect, as was previously illustrated in the PCM Model.

Textual Mapping and Legends

There is absolutely no doubt that information design and knowledge mapping—which may be thought of as a form of textual cartography, with texts, images, commentaries, etc.—will affect and shape society significantly. The scientist today is also a knowledge architect, who has to face both the challenge and responsibility for mapping vast information territories, which will progressively expand according to preset foundations.

Any topographic model is based upon a certain geographic theory. Whether the theory is grounded in a Ptolemaic system of reference, a Newtonian one, or a Copernican one, it deeply affects mapping criteria, which then reflect upon the final result. In the same way, for accurate mapping of information within a text, not only is it crucial to make an initial decision about the amount of information to be represented, but it is also important to acknowledge the theory behind what is being represented to be able to proceed toward consistent planning and accurate design. Just as geographic maps may represent different aspects of the same territory, information maps meant to be for texts will have to be designed so that they describe what they are meant to convey. They will respond to different possible users' modes of navigating them for different purposes and with different criteria.

Just as geographical maps reflect the technological level of a certain society and its knowledge and perception of the world itself, information maps will reflect very precise kinds of interpretation through new technological tools. New theories will open up the possibility of seeing what was invisible before because it had not been mapped. Some theories of information and interpretation may lead to extremely valuable tools for surface identification of textual regions, whereas other theories acting at a more conceptual level may be needed like some kinds of thermal infrared photographs to reveal ground temperature patterns (Biddle, Milne, and Shortle 1974). The same principle applies to the possibility of identifying different sources of information pollution. These may be reframed in terms of first recognizing and then isolating some distorted information originating from a specific point that must be recognized within a certain territory.

With CPP-TRS, a further layer for consistent interpretation of specific and precise textual features in relation to other features is added. Those features were first identified and then named the "communicative positioning." Having introduced specific icons for each positioning feature (which may be isolated or in combination) implies the need to make a legend available to the reader very much like geographical legends based on conventional signs. Textual maps are therefore conceived as derivative texts out of an originating text, having undergone a certain process or a set of processes. As with maps, they are intended to be used for specific purposes, as they represent symbolic versions of the actual text from which they have been derived. As such, they work on a quantitatively reduced text, resulting in a qualitatively enhanced model of the text itself at a highly specific level of abstraction. A textual map is conceived not as mere reproduction of the text to be represented; it will result in a manageable abstraction of the spatial distribution of previously selected positioning features. A textual map may also complement other criteria that have been used for commenting on a text by adding value to any kind of mapping that has previously been designed. Any CPP-TRS-based mapping model will, in addition, help eliminate noise or distraction within the mapping system, both on the mapmaker's and on the map user's side, where noise is precisely that kind of interference that may prevent a concept from reaching the reader. In mapping texts, just as in mapping territories, it is absolutely important to make sure that the "channel capacity" does not become saturated by too much detail or too much noise. This means that if mapping becomes too thick, if information is too dense, the reader may become overwhelmed and lose or lower active reaction to new information.

Some noise in textual mapping may derive from the addition of information that may not be directly relevant to the function being explicated by the map itself. Some noise may be generated by the textual map designer and may be reduced significantly in the course of accurate revision processes. Noise in textual mapmaking will also reflect upon map navigation and perception. Because both textual maps and legends refer to different categories of symbols, schemes, and icons, collision and collapsing may occur in graphic representation unless accurate design is carefully and thoroughly planned and carried out, thus directing perception by progressive adjustment and readjustment phases.

A textual map is therefore a symbolic representation of a text. It reflects and indicates those properties the textual map designer perceives as most fundamental within a certain text. The designer has to decide which properties are relevant according to a consistent and consensually agreed upon model, which has been planned to facilitate the map reader and made compatible with a set of possible kinds of expected use. Any textual map will by definition reduce the actual text in very precisely predefined and highly selective ways, just as scales in maps indicate.

Such reduction will therefore impose another specific and well-defined limitation on the use and further interpretation of the originating and consistently mapped text.

Any textual map will have to indicate "the scale of reduction" that had been adopted. A model is an interpretive device meant to help understand a more or less complex system. The more complex the system, the more articulated the model will have to be. Statically designed models may have to become dynamic to show those aspects that would otherwise be missing. Linear representation systems may have to be turned into three-dimensional models to express aspects that would otherwise be lost. Many levels of complexity that are observed and identified may have to be turned into three-layered representation systems to be fully exploited.

Textual maps and other textual models are strictly dependent upon the actual text they are planned to represent. They also have to produce a breakthrough and provide insights into deeper understanding of each text that has been previously analyzed and consistently processed to identify the noise that needs to be removed. What is significant information versus what is actually disturbing noise depends strictly upon the kind of texts under investigation, the kind of problems that have been previously addressed, and the personal judgment of the investigator. Textual maps and textual models represent incomplete abstraction processes because they refer to a very limited set of aspects reflecting upon texts, where the scale limits and at the same time explicates the amount of detail carried out. Textual maps are also related to the specific time in which they are produced and are therefore static. Because they are designed for a specific purpose, they also show a certain level of subjectivity according to the mapmaker's decision. Subjectivity is in any case limited by the fact that a consensually shared and agreed-upon system for interpretation is used.

A mapmaker applying the theory of text comprehension will implicitly allow some more subjective interpretation attribution by assuming responsibility, whereas a system applying the theory of text compression will be more precise and somehow deterministic, just as mathematical models in mapmaking are more precise than diagrammatic ones. As for any model referring to a continuously changing and expanding reality, effectiveness of textual maps will change over time according to new information that is to be added and reorganized. Textual maps, like well-designed models, may be predictive in the sense that they may be used as a basis for decision making and planning of new texts, though many variables may be left out. Textual maps do summarize consistently selected information about the originating text in a highly structured way, therefore suggesting new paths for further investigation of actual texts within a certain knowledge domain. Textual maps are also a reduction of a real text and result in a generalized representation of it.

Textual mapping is based on progressive expansion and is therefore dynamic by nature because new versions of the same text or updated or new texts are coming in all the time. Nevertheless, major mapping operations should be undertaken upon complex but relatively stabilized information territories. Textual mapping is not only appropriate at a descriptive level, but at an operational level as well. The consistency of the model will guarantee that those results may be obtained that were planned originally.

Redefined Terminology and Lexicon

This lexicon is meant to define the terms introduced and used in the newly established theoretical framework of the physics of language.

Aspect: a possible way to regard or view a certain communicative phenomenon taking place in one of the possible states of information.

Conductivity: the property or power of conducting communicative function, communicative intention, and communicative turn-taking carried by each textual unit. (See *Conductor.*)

Conductor: a metalanguage, in the physics of language represented by CPP-TRS, able to conduct communicative function, communicative intention, and communicative turn-taking. (See *Conductivity.*)

Configuration: the relative disposition or arrangement of parts or elements of a text resulting in an external and more global textual form. (See *Reconfiguration.*)

Continuous (flow of information): information flow that shows up as uninterrupted in time without cessation and in immediate connection or spatial relationship, resulting in a continuous information territory. (See *Discontinuous Flow of Information.*)

Conversion: the act or process of converting a text and the state of being converted, implying a physical transformation from one information state into another. The global transformation of language material into an iconized set of simplified strings. (See *Converter.*)

Converter: the CPP-TRS device for information conversion, meaning an interpretation device alternating communicative current to direct current and vice versa. (See *Conversion.*)

CPP-TRS Compiler: a computer program that may translate a textual pentagram into a textual hologram. (See *Textual Hologram.*)

Degree: any of a set of steps in either processing or retrogressing a text, both globally and locally represented by different points in a scale. A unit of measure, as of information pressure, marked off consistently on the scale of a measuring instrument. (See *Step.*)

Direct: the process of managing and guiding information-seeking through direct use of CPP-TRS instructions, regulating the course of events and actions and channelling or focusing toward a certain information target. (See *Redirect.*)

Discontinuous (flow of information): Interrupted in time and even intermittent flow of information, missing some immediate connection or spatial relationship, resulting in a discontinuous information territory if not accurately processed. (See *Continuous Flow of Information.*)

Electric textual charge: in the physics of language, one of the basic properties of textual segments generating interactions of different kinds through energy. (See *Electric Textual Current.*)

Electric textual current: the time rate of flow of electric textual charge channeled toward a predefined direction. (See *Electric Textual Charge.*)

Engine: CPP-TRS considered as a device that converts one of several forms of communicative energy to be applied to texts as to enhance text processing in different ways and for different aspects, more precisely for text interpretation and text understanding. (See *Propeller.*)

Granularity: discontinuity of density in knowledge and information matter to be extended to language matter as well; showing an alternation of filled-in and empty spaces within one same information territory.

Interference: in the physics of language is meant to be the process in which two or more closely linked communicative functions or communicative intentions may combine to reinforce or cancel each other; the final communicative effect of the close interaction being the result of the interplay.

Mode: a specific communicative disposition showing very precise and essential properties reflecting directly upon sentence and paragraph structure in each language. (See *Position.*)

Position: specific condition of a text with reference to communicative function, communicative intention, and communicative turn-taking. (See *Mode.*)

Progression: the act of progressing from a certain textual stage toward a more advanced stage involving a better "textual resolution." (See *Retrogression.*)

Propagation: the act of propagating information by causing it to multiply, to reproduce itself, to create a communicative effect at distance, or to increase in extent. (See *Stabilization.*)

Propeller: CPP-TRS considered as a device working on a three-component base to provide text generation energy. (See *Engine.*)

Reconfiguration: the change and remodeling of the relative disposition or arrangement of parts or elements of a text resulting in a new external and more global textual form. (See *Configuration.*)

Redirect: the process of changing information-seeking by modifying CPP-TRS instructions, therefore redirecting and refocusing toward a different information target. (See *Direct.*)

Restitution: reparation made on a text by creating an equivalent replacement compensating for some previous loss occurred, mostly showing a different but consistent style. (See *Restoration.*)

Restoration: a return of a text or part of a text in the form of one or more sentences and one or more paragraphs to a former condition or restitution of one or more sentences or paragraphs taken away or lost; reconstruction or reproduction of specific context, showing in its original state and with its original style. (See *Restitution.*)

Retrogression: the act of passing from a more advanced and complex textual stage to an earlier or simpler, in any case less advanced, state. (See *Progression.*)

Revision: the act of amending or altering parts of a text in the form of a sentence or sentences and a paragraph or paragraphs in order to improve original text resolution or to update it.

Stability: the quality of being stable even if of a relatively certain information territory. (See *Stabilization.*)

Stabilization: the act or process of stabilizing or the state of being stabilized of a certain information territory, still a relative concept because information territories are subject to update or expansion though at different speed. (See *Stability.*)

Step: the positioning movement on a local level that may result in repositioning at a global level. Each positioning movement will cover just the distance measured by such positioning movement. (See *Degree.*)

Structure: the result of information planning, design, and knowledge building for text construction, arrangement of parts, and constituents for precise function. (See *Structured Programming.*)

Structured Programming: the design and coding of programming techniques by a methodology (CPP-TRS) that successively breaks textual problems into smaller and nested textual subunits. (See *Structure.*)

Textual Engineering: the art or science of making practical applications of such pure sciences as physics and chemistry of language in the construction of textual buildings.

Textual Hologram: in the optics of text, a high resolution textual pentagram exposed to coherent three-dimensional light reflecting communicative function, communicative intention, and communicative turn-taking. (See *CPP-TRS Compiler.*)

Turbid: an output text resulting from turbulent conditions or characterized by lack of clarity and transparency because of the sediment's outgrowth, opacity, and obscuration. Exceeding thickness or density of information resulting in confused and disturbed textual resolution. (See *Turbulence.*)

Turbulence: the quality or state of information in agitation or tumult, given fuzzy and uncontrolled information flows. (See *Turbid.*)

Vanishing: the act of causing to disappear or the state of disappearing of textual information previously vaporized. (See *Vaporization.*)

Vaporization: the act of vaporizing or the state of being vaporized of textual information destined to disappear after change of communicative pressure has occurred. (See *Vanishing.*)

3

Photos

Chris Ehrmann

Figure 3.1. The Union Station Indoor Model (The USI Model). © Chris Ehrmann

Figure 3.2. The Union Station Outdoor Model (The USO Model). © Chris Ehrmann

Figure 3.3. The Union Station Outdoor Model (The USO Model). © *Chris Ehrmann*

Figure 3.4. The Union Station Outdoor Model (The USO Model). © *Chris Ehrmann*

Figure 3.5. National Gallery of Art Model. © Chris Ehrmann

Figure 3.6. National Gallery of Art Model. © Chris Ehrmann

Figure 3.7. National Air and Space Museum Model. © Chris Ehrmann

Figure 3.8. Hirshorn Museum Model. © Chris Ehrmann

Figure 3.9. The Museum of African Art & The Arthur Sackler Gallery & The Dillon Ripley Center Model (The Museum of African Art). © Chris Ehrmann

Figure 3.10. The Museum of African Art & The Arthur Sackler Gallery & The Dillon Ripley Center Model (Arthur M. Sackler Gallery). © Chris Ehrmann

Figure 3.11. The Museum of African Art & The Arthur Sackler Gallery & The Dillon Ripley Center Model (S. Dillon Ripley Center). © Chris Ehrmann

4

Basic Principles of Information Design

The Walter Gropius Chair

Phase 1

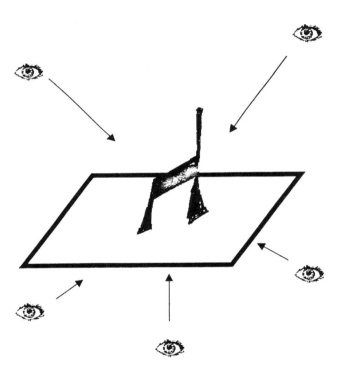

The Walter Gropius Chair

Phase 2

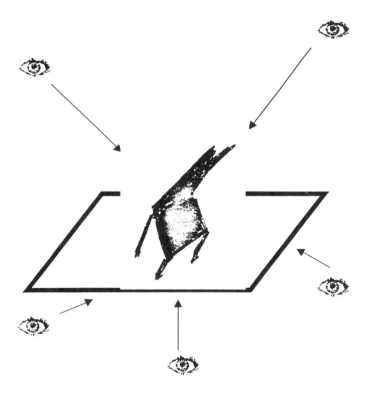

Unprocessed?

Processed?

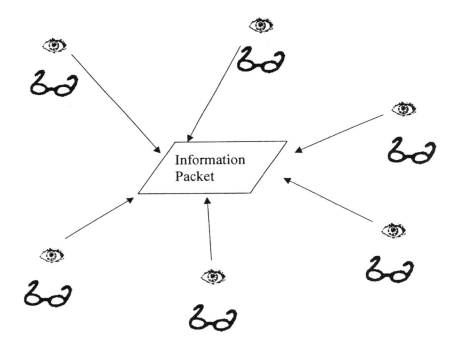

Information
Packet

Multifaceted
Viewing

Augmented View of a certain object

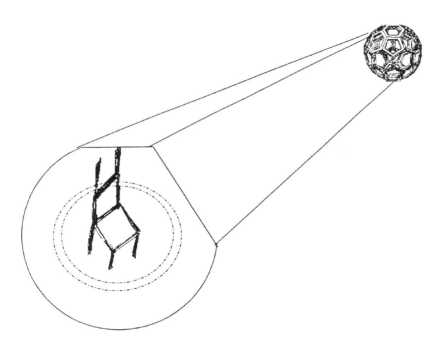

Augmented View of Information

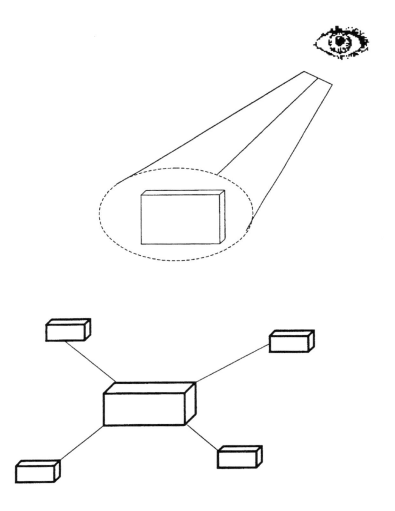

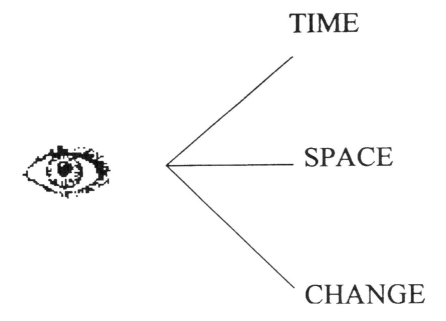

Envisioning Information is a complex process which may be
effectively supported by

Metaphorical and Analogical Reasoning

Both in metaphors and analogies design, it is most important
to have:

❑ Accuracy: To what extent does the metaphor or analogy
apply?

❑ Visibility: Which are the relevant features?

❑ Progression: How does one domain get close to another
one?

❑ Consistency: How does one domain reflect upon another
one?

❑ Continuity: How to progress from one domain toward
another one without disconnecting the analogical reasoning
process?

A consistent theoretical framework will positively reflect upon effective ways of planning and designing information and of building knowledge

Aerial view on the complexity of each task

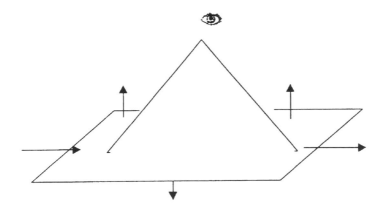

Information territory to undergo construction

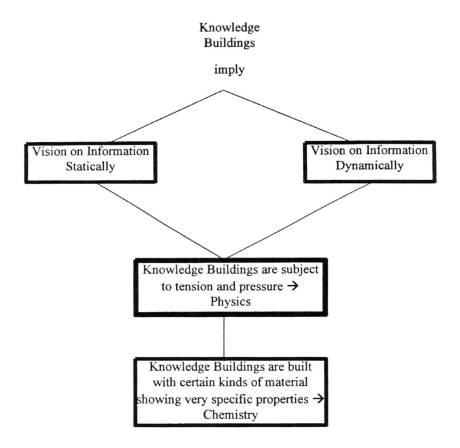

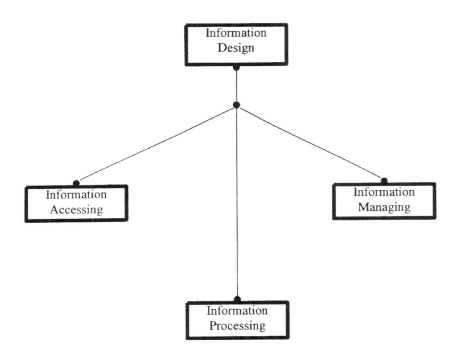

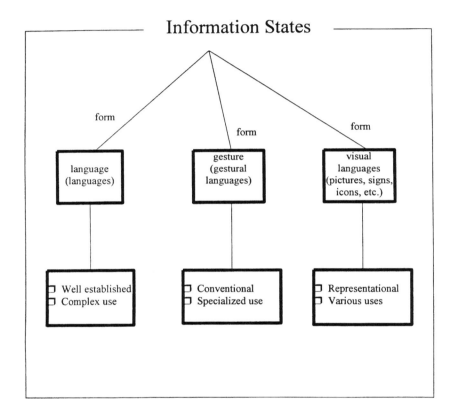

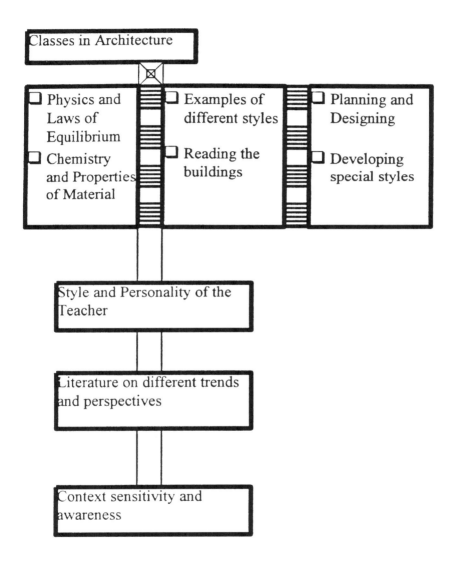

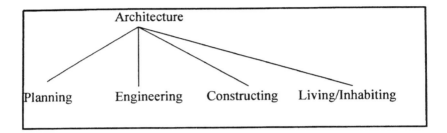

Just like in architecture, the way the overall process is organized and arranged will deeply influence people's lives...

....the way information is designed will deeply affect people's learning and knowledge accessing capabilities....therefore deeply influencing life as well....

When information conveyed via natural language hits the different media....then

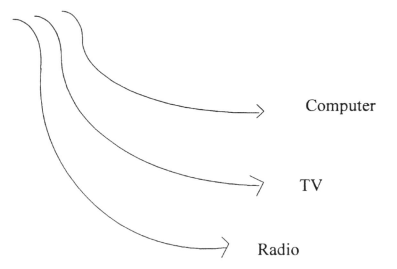

Computer

TV

Radio

it is subject to different perceptive reactions.

Natural language is in fact very delicate and highly context-sensitive.

There are Different Degrees of Elaboration in Processing and Packaging Knowledge

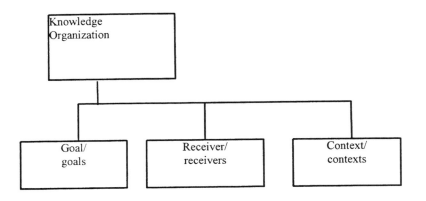

Skills to be developed: how to become knowledgeable and skilled therefore able to turn information into knowledge by promoting awareness and context-sensitivity.

MACRO INFORMATION DESIGN

❑ Planning

❑ Decision Making

MICRO INFORMATION DESIGN

❑ Planning

❑ Decision Making

**Communication Environmental Awareness
is concerned with issues such as:**

❑ how to integrate information resources harmoniously;

❑ how to combine different communication tools and make them
    compatible;

❑ how to create a high context-sensitivity in order to be able to
    plan consistently on "information territories" and on
    "knowledge buildings";

❑ how to coordinate actions to be taken by sharing a common
    terminology meant to transmit very precise instructions.

Information Design
needs to be based upon

Visions on Information in a very broad sense.
Only this way will it be possible to proceed toward
organization of a whole information territory, with
different tools, different functionalities, different
materials and different individuals involved in the
planning and the actual construction.

Nature of the information material to be processed:

1. Stable information (which degree of stability?)

2. Stabilized knowledge (which time and frequency of use?)

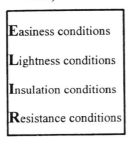

Easiness conditions

Lightness conditions

Insulation conditions

Resistance conditions

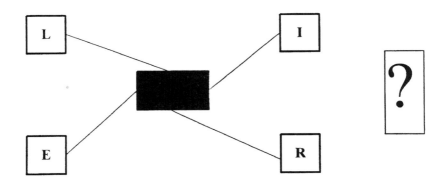

It is absolutely important to create a set of relational evaluation systems so as to decide at each given time which choice should be made

Before any construction may actually get started, the site will need to be carefully measured and prepared.

Construction workers will know what to do from blueprints prepared by architects and engineers.

Part of the workers' training is knowing how to read blueprints.

Specialized tools for building are needed so that construction is possible upon accurate excavation, which means digging the hole for the foundation and basement.

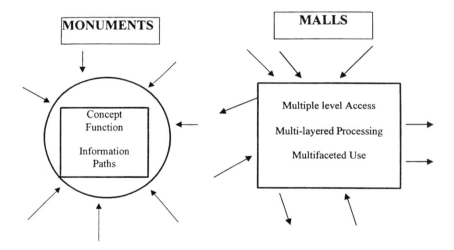

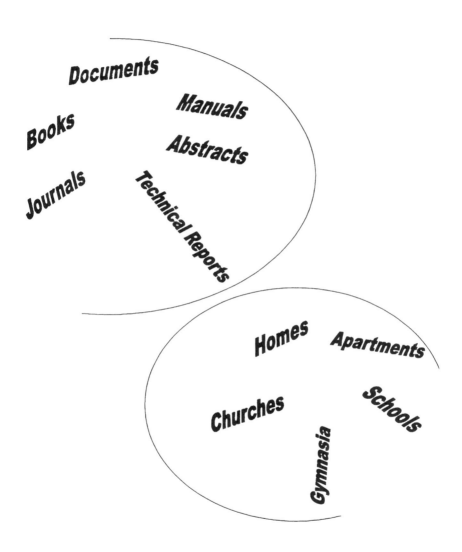

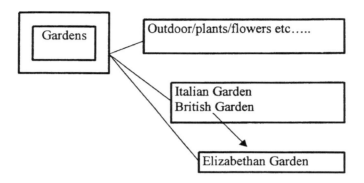

Organization of built and nonbuilt areas –

produces   ⟶

Vision of spaces, both inhabited and not inhabited –

where   ⟶

Living conditions are created by building conditions -

Only once rules and constraints determined by physical properties of information matter are known, as well as specific properties about composition of information states and possible vs. impossible combinations, may we actually think of expressing different and personal styles in designing information.

Information Design is conceived here as deriving from a strong theoretical background about the nature of information from which experience-based guidelines may be derived too.

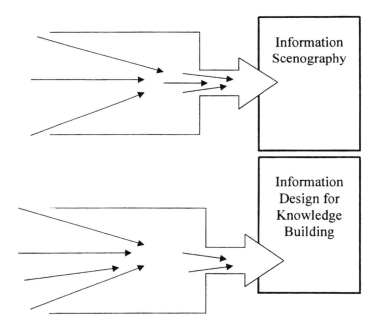

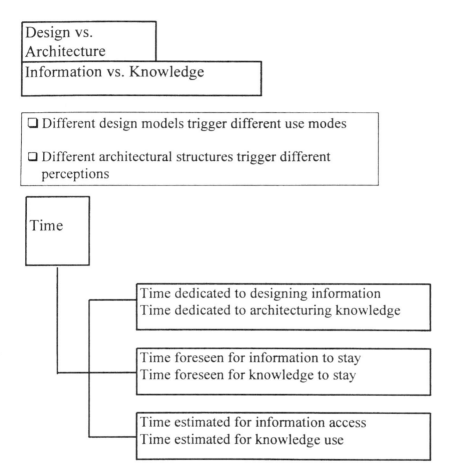

Design vs.
Architecture
Information vs. Knowledge

❑ Different design models trigger different use modes

❑ Different architectural structures trigger different
   perceptions

Time

Time dedicated to designing information
Time dedicated to architecturing knowledge

Time foreseen for information to stay
Time foreseen for knowledge to stay

Time estimated for information access
Time estimated for knowledge use

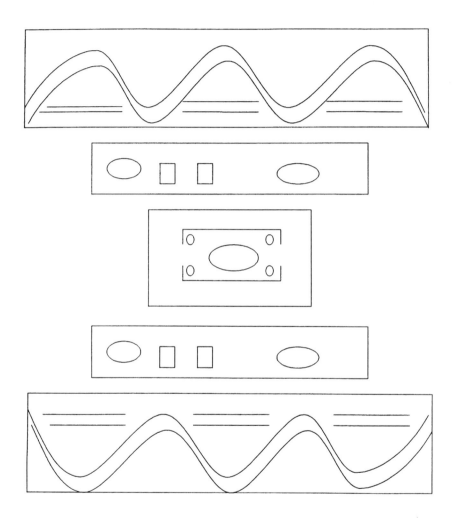

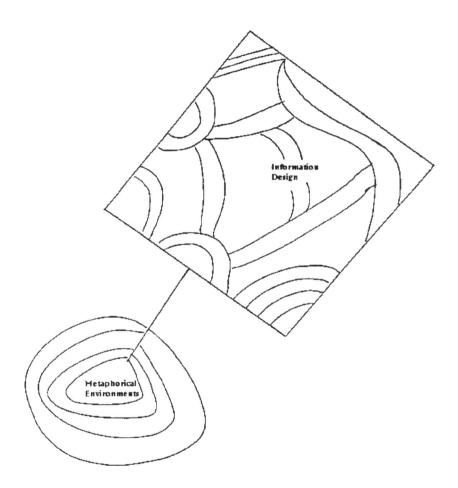

Information
Design

Metaphorical
Environments

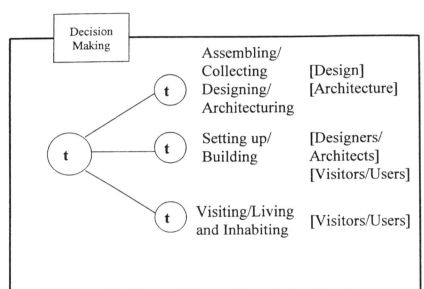

Different decision making on time choices implies different decision making on design setups, architectural models and kinds of material (language/icons...), which do in any case affect the overall perception.

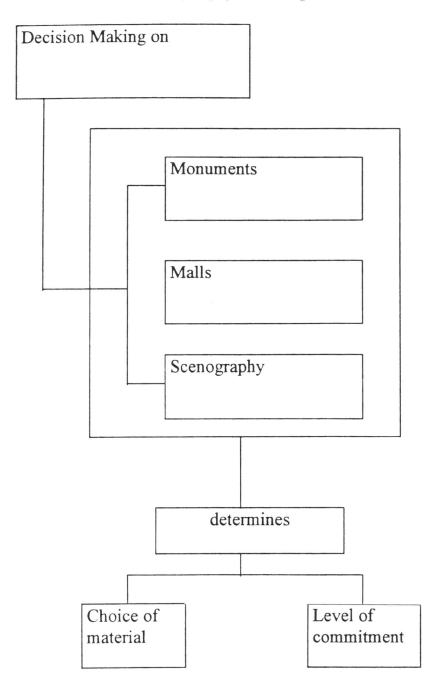

Permanent
Functionality
Buildings

Monuments

❑ Suggested paths;
❑ Knowledge
    background.

❑ Some internal change and
  path options possible;
❑ Basic Stability.

Semipermanent Functionality
Buildings

Malls

❑ Free paths;
❑ Structural information
  distribution stability;
❑ Possible change/update/
  revision

Access and acquisition for more
or less immediate use.
Possible internal restructuring
and refunctionalizing.

Temporary Functionality
Scenography and Set Ups

Theatrical
Scenography
Exhibits Set Ups

❑ Special information setting
  providing more or less close
  relationships between actor
  and audience;
❑ Different degrees of active
  versus passive behavior.

Flexibility of use.
Possibility of different projection
degrees.

<u>Textual Scenography</u>   is the art of representing a
document on a perspective
plan reflecting one or more
specific point or points of
view and not on a principal
interpretation axis – It is
therefore considered to be the
art of perspective
representation applied to the
organization and
representation of stage
cooperative working
scenarios.

<u>Orthographic Projection</u>   being the specific technique
and set of techniques meant to
focus on a specific point
desired or set of specific
points desired.

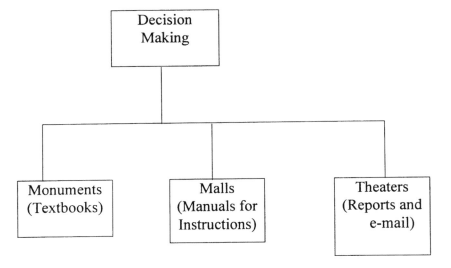

Information Design is about:

❑ Promoting qualitative reasoning about communication and information.

❑ Promoting quantitative measurement and qualitative criteria for information processing.

❑ Promoting context sensitivity.

❑ Promoting "in depth search" capabilities and "in breadth search" capabilities.

❑ Promoting cognitive awareness about the different tools and media.

❑ Promoting "Macrodesign" skills and "Microdesign" skills.

❑ Promoting knowledge of the Physics and Chemistry of information.

First decision making	Text for mass production	**?**
	Text handcrafted	**?**

The greatest difference between the designer and the single independent craftsperson is that the craftsperson does not face the problem of communicating his or her intentions to others for translation into objects.

The designer, however, must make his or her intentions explicit and communication is at the heart of industrial design.

Designers do not manufacture things; they think, they analyze, they may model, draw and specify.

All good designers ask questions to their clients and spend time helping the client clarify what he or she really wants.

Old distinction between designers and engineers

"Designers differ from engineers in that engineers though may proceed intuitively, prefer to test, whereas an industrial designer is entirely happy with intuitive judgments. But unlike an engineer, a designer is not responsible for the structural failure of the final product and output."

There exists a very widely spread and commonly perceived need to create a quasi-scientific basis for Design.

New products → New materials → New styles

"In the 1940's, furniture designers were excited by the possibilities offered by new laminates, new bending techniques and combinations of laminated wood, metal and plastic."

Interesting Reading about the Designer Mentality:

Donner, P., 1993, Design since 1965, Thames and Hudson, London

| Paul Roberts | "Virtual Grub Street" (June 1996-Cincinnati, OH - Harper's Magazine - reproduced by 1997 Writer's Yearbook) pp. 22 ff. "Special Issue" |

"Writers needn't be experts so much as filters whose task is to absorb and compress great gobs of information into small, easily digestible on-screen chunks". p. 22

"Non linearity, we are told, redistributes narrative power to readers". p. 23

"A new literary form?" p. 23

"Multimedia Writers?" p. 24

Specific writing skills and context sensitivity as well as effective filtering attitudes need to be developed.

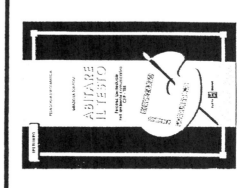

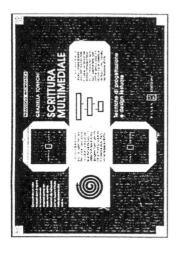

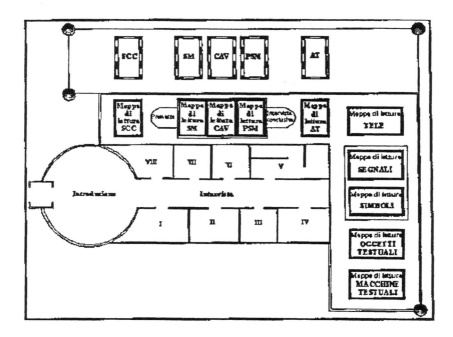

In Information Design
Creativity and Preciseness need
to go together

Creativity is – also –
access to
different scripts
and
capability to
pass from one
to another one.

Preciseness is – also –
definition of the kind of
access to the combination
of different scripts and
capability to focus on
some features and aspects
as opposed to all of them.

Wordwork: appropriate and accurate
use of technical
terminology is meant to
describe and define
processes and events and
to make consistent
interpretation of blueprints
possible.

Open and dynamic patterns to be used in a flexible but extremely accurate way.

Qualitative reasoning about information.

Common sense knowledge about communication.

Cognitive fingertips and cognitive fingerprints.

The standardgraph metaphor is a powerful one to allow representation of qualitative aspects being measured quantitatively too.

"By analyzing carefully new ways to better define a new field such as Information Design (ID) is, I can see some need to discuss some basic terminology and basic concepts coming from Economics, which may be productively adapted to ID, of course only after accurate reformulation.

As to be able to create some common background for discussion, I can first of all foresee the need to create a distinction between Micro Information Design issues and Macro Information Design issues just like Micro Economics and Macro Economics do have different though highly compatible concerns.

Micro Information Design can be defined as that branch of Information Processing which is in fact concerned specifically with individual information units and knowledge packages. Macro Information Design is concerned with the behavior of aggregate information variables, through the study of information activities and processes of various and different kinds, taken as an interdependent and interconnected whole and dynamically represented in their differentiated stages too."

Just like Economics, Information Design is meant to be a science that analyzes different allocation and utilization of information resources and most of the time choices need to be made without the complete data spectrum available and because of major time and costs concerns, they are therefore made out of projection and prediction. Less efficiency may sometimes be preferred to increase or keep established relations, which would otherwise be jeopardized. This is precisely where qualitative reasoning and quantitative analysis and measurement come in as an effective need.

Cognitive Fingertips and
Cognitive Fingerprints

Be very cautious when you decompress information!
Passing from a certain state, the compressed one, into
another, the decompressed one, too rapidly may
affect the perception because of the quantity
overload.

(The Microwave and Frozen Pie Example)

Create as much structure as needed in packaging
knowledge! Too much structure may result in
undesirable constraints, whereas visibility may
require moving around without hitting heavily
constraining and rigid barriers.

(The Chairs and Window Example)

The Microwave and Frozen Pie Example

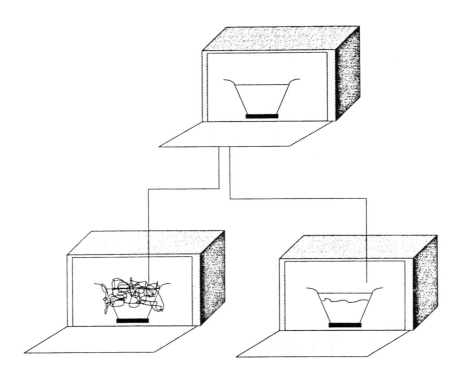

The Chairs and Window Example

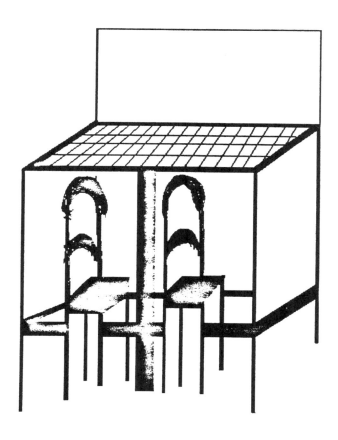

Whenever major flows of information are in the process of getting organized and reconfigured as knowledge packages, a set of EVENTS is likely to occur.

If they are well known in advance, they are then more likely to be monitored and turned into highly effective processes.

This is why a specific and complex competence allowing for communicative patterns recognition as well as for qualitative reasoning needs to be developed: competence being "the quality or state of being adequate or of having sufficient knowledge, judgment, skills or strength in a certain field". (Webster's Dictionary)

EVENTS which may be turned into PROCESSES
and harmoniously monitored

Dissemination: the process of distributing knowledge packages
                 widely, meaning in small particles and
                 everywhere.

Dispersion: the process of spreading information over a wide
                 area after selective separation of a non-
                 homogeneous information emission in accordance
                 with some characteristics (speed – energy –
                 wavelength – particle mass).

Dissipation: the process of spreading information in random
                 ways to the point of destroying an original
                 information territory identity.

Distortion: the process of altering or twisting an original and
                 natural condition in information territories.

Diffusion: the process of deliberately causing to spread
                 around according to a preset series of tasks and
                 targets.

Disruption: the process of breaking apart, through an
                 interruption meant to prevent normal continuance,
                 therefore deeply affecting and destroying the
                 unity or wholeness.

Distribution: the process of dividing knowledge packages
                 among several tasks and targets according to
                 different categories.

Dissolution: the process of separation between and among
                      knowledge packages entailing loss of connections,
                      previously active.

Disintegration: the process of separation into component parts
                      affecting the global structure of information
                      territories and causing transformations at different
                      levels and various degrees.

Distillation: the process of driving off gas from solids,
                      meaning extracting abstract concepts out of
                      knowledge packages producing for purification
                      purposes the formation of new information
                      substances like conceptual chains and title
                      condensed sequences.

Distinction: the process of separating into parts different
                      information territories after having assigned a
                      topical target and topical tasks too.

Dilution: the process of deliberate reduction in the
                      informative value of all information territory.

Dissociation: the process by which a strongly bound
                      combination of knowledge packages breaks up
                      into simpler constituents capable of recombining
                      under certain conditions.

With such radical changes occurring within our current time and space framework, how could we actually think of language and communication the same way we used to do before?

Information transport, which means precisely passing from written texts in their stabilized form, like currently used textbooks and journal articles, into a hypertext format or according to website standards will entail a deep and quite articulated rethinking, which will trigger major changes as well.

We are in fact able to see a "Doppler-like effect" in text perception and processing, which is an apparent shift in the frequency of communication waves received by an observer and text perceiver, depending on relative motion between the observer and text perceiver and the source text generated communicative waves.

Information Design

Information Design: Methodologies
Information Design: Current Trends
Information Design: Tonfoni's Perspective
Information Design: History of the Field
Information Design: Contemporary
Information Design: Thoughts and Ways of Thinking
Information Design: The Lexicon
Information Design: The Tools
Information Design: Qualitative Reasoning
Information Design: Quantitative Parameters and
                     Measurements or Informetrics

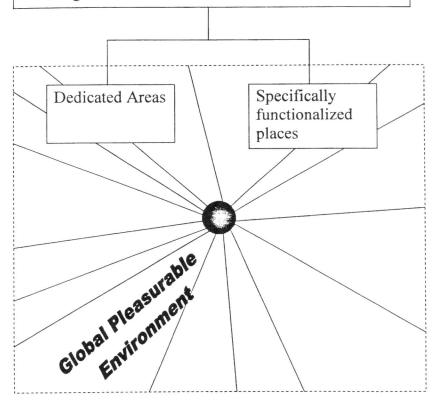

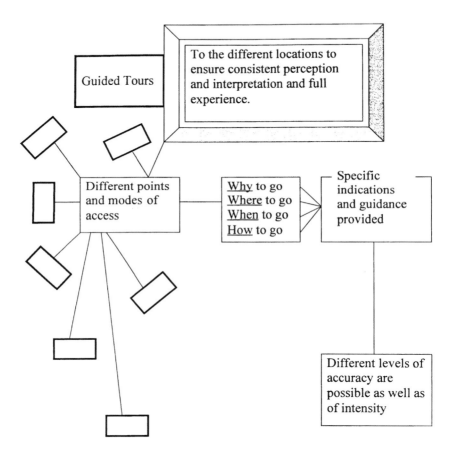

Guided Tours

To the different locations to ensure consistent perception and interpretation and full experience.

Different points and modes of access

Why to go
Where to go
When to go
How to go

Specific indications and guidance provided

Different levels of accuracy are possible as well as of intensity

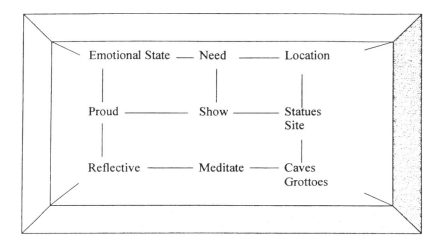

Typography/Characters	Emotional States
Formatting/Editing	Information Needs
Concerns/Solutions	Information Territories/ Knowledge Buildings

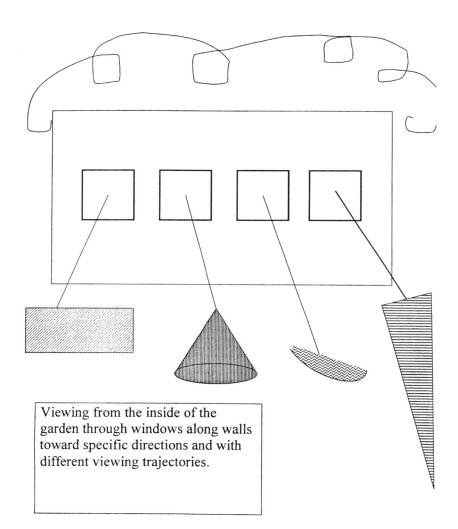

Viewing from the inside of the
garden through windows along walls
toward specific directions and with
different viewing trajectories.

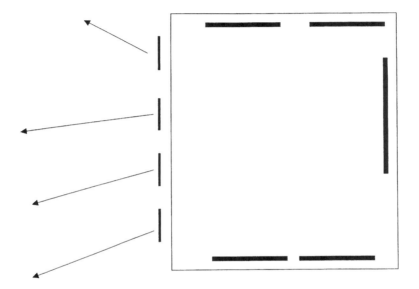

Spatial and time-related reasoning about Information Design related to the perception that is planned and meant to be achieved.

Information Design/
Knowledge Building

PROBLEM DEFINITION

You need to define accurately the
information/knowledge problem as to
be able to conceptualize it and
visualize it sharply and consistently.

You need to prioritize and then focus
on main aspects and make sure that all
the derivative decisions and choices
are consistent.

In breadth search for most suitable
metaphorical environment.

In depth search for
most appropriate
features to be
selected and
accurately worked
out and reframed.

Harmoniously evolving knowledge buildings construction implies accurate decision making upon:

❑ Continuity vs. discontinuity within the pre-selected information territory;

❑ Consistency in the tight relationship existing between the kind of material and the style, means between knowledge and knowledge packaging modes;

❑ Selection between homogeneous and dishomogeneous knowledge.

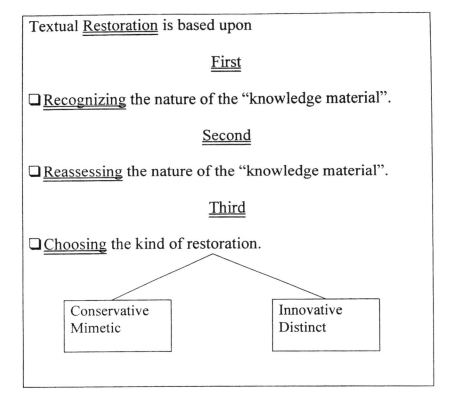

Textual <u>Restoration</u> is based upon

<u>First</u>

❏ <u>Recognizing</u> the nature of the "knowledge material".

<u>Second</u>

❏ <u>Reassessing</u> the nature of the "knowledge material".

<u>Third</u>

❏ <u>Choosing</u> the kind of restoration.

| Conservative Mimetic | Innovative Distinct |

A Few Basic Hints for Accurate Building

❑ Isolate the most crucial problem.

❑ Identify the most accessible level.

❑ Create the most consistent metaphor.

❑ Foresee and represent all possible evolutions.

❑ Anticipate possible endangering factors and resistance.

❑ Plan consistently and dynamically.

ADDRESS THE CRUCIAL POINTS AND QUESTIONS

Where does the information flow actually start from (?)

Where does it stop now (?)

Will it continue (?)

Toward which direction (?)

REFLECTING UPON

Where should the manual/software actually
start and end?

Size/Shape/Structure
of the
Knowledge Building
Estimate

It is very important to develop a special
sensitivity to information problems such as:

❑ Where does the information flow start and stop now?

❑ Which dynamic flows of information should be
converted into well organized information territories
or knowledge buildings of various kinds?

❑ Which flows of information are more likely to stop or
continue?

Departure point: envisioning the
information flow.

Check quantity and quality of information through both
evaluative and strategic reasoning.

Parameters

continuous – discontinuous
connected – disconnected
homogeneous – dishomogeneous
verified – unverified
up-to-date – to be updated
upgraded – to be upgraded

Envisioning the past-present-future of the construction

Relevant questions to be asked to support evaluative and strategic reasoning:

❑ Where did the information flow get started?

❑ How did the information flow get started?

❑ For how long did the information flow continue?

❑ How many operators have been involved in the process?

❑ For how long have operators been involved in the process?

❑ Which role did the operators actually play?

❑ Which kind of planning of the construction was made?

❑ Did the actual design reflect the original planning?

❑ Did the actual implementation reflect the design and the planning?

❑ Which changes and/or near misses may be recognized and why were they made?

Knowledge Statics

Knowledge Dynamics

If a physical approach toward language and information and knowledge building is introduced, then many variables do come into play, such as SPACE and TIME.

Information organization and knowledge building need therefore to be targeted toward highly specific goal achievement and be referred to different kinds of time and space variables.

Time (and times) of perception as well as Space (and spaces) of perception should also be foreseen and handled in multiple and different ways.

Accurate Information Design

and

Consistent Knowledge Building

may be

ENVISIONED
VIEWED
VISUALIZED

in many different ways, which may facilitate
ACCURATE PERCEPTION and CONSISTENT
PROCESSING and INTERPRETATION.

Just like the very same object may be
observed from different perspectives
and points of view and therefore be
perceived in multiple ways.

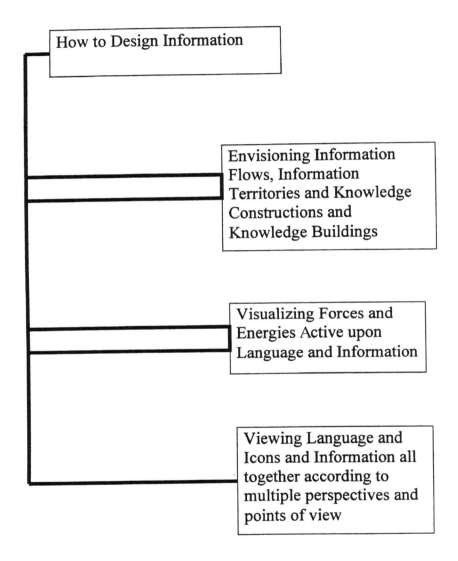

Envisioning: Meant specifically for
architectural models evolving in
space and time, information flows
to be then organized as
information territories.

The planning process shows to be
particularly useful and a high
degree of accuracy may be
reached thanks to technical
capacity and mastering of both
simple and complex techniques.

Viewing: meant specifically for both simple
                      and complex objects, structures
                      and textures and to be linked
                      directly to architectural,
                      photographic and pictorial
                      perception.

                      The dynamically evolving process
                      of viewing shows to be effective
                      in order to distinguish and
                      represent multiple levels and
                      layers and to recreate holographic
                      configuration in language and in
                      communication.

Visualizing: meant specifically for identifying, defining, representing and exploring elements, which were previously unidentified, after having had them surface.

The progressive observation and analysis process, just like in physics and chemistry, allows for definition and description of different kinds of phenomena, in space and time and at different levels of complexity.

Models for Information Design need to be performed
and executed according to a specific set of
instructions and depending on the kind of use, which
has been planned at each given time.

Models in Information Design are both

COMPLEX
and
DYNAMIC

The concept of "model performance" or "model
execution" derives directly from the more global
concept of "complex and dynamic conceptual
environment", which may be only partially activated
and handled according to specific priorities set up at
each given time.

A complex model is not a fuzzy model; complexity does in fact entail a high degree of accuracy and precision.

In order to be properly handled, those different layers and levels need in fact to be first isolated and recognized and defined, then to be prioritized, selected and progressively ordered as to allow for final and most appropriate performance and execution of the model to actually take place.

On Building "new" knowledge buildings
On Restoring "old" knowledge buildings

Identify the "information territory"-
Visit the "information territory"-

Choose the suitable "knowledge material"-
Choose the available "knowledge material"-

Select techniques for planning and building -
Decide techniques for restoration and completion -

Plan accurately for integration of "present" and "future" -
Plan accurately for integration of "past" and "present" -

Plan on space and time needed for future construction -
Recognize/analyze space and time needed in the already
available construction -

Plan on functionalities to be "built in" -
Verify the already existing and "built in" functionalities -

Viollet Le Duc carefully explored and studied the relationship existing between the kind of material and the finally resulting building, with specific attention paid to technical details.

Gaudí proceeded toward extension and expansion of previously organized models available in the architectural studies tradition of his country and not only.

Relevant questions to be answered were:

❑ which "models" should be selected and for what reasons;

❑ how a "single style" should reflect upon "collective style" and how eclecticism still will have single authors;

❑ how the "new tradition" should be linked to the "old tradition" and be recognized in its own features;

❑ how "complexity", "contradictions", "dynamicity", "continuity" and "diversity" need to be combined and in which ways should different models reflect different users' needs.

Modernism

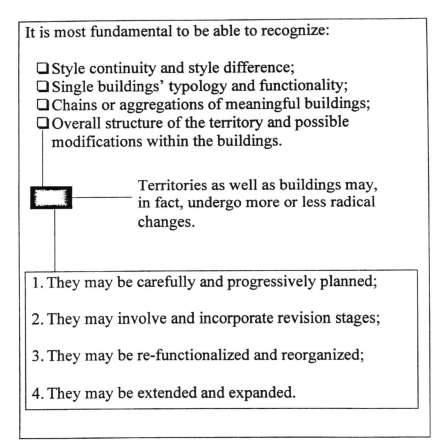

It is most fundamental to be able to recognize:

❑ Style continuity and style difference;
❑ Single buildings' typology and functionality;
❑ Chains or aggregations of meaningful buildings;
❑ Overall structure of the territory and possible
   modifications within the buildings.

Territories as well as buildings may, in fact, undergo more or less radical changes.

1. They may be carefully and progressively planned;

2. They may involve and incorporate revision stages;

3. They may be re-functionalized and reorganized;

4. They may be extended and expanded.

▲Why should a certain KNOWLEDGE BUILDING be RESTORED or RESTRUCTURED?

▲Why should a certain KNOWLEDGE OBJECT be REASSEMBLED or RECONFIGURED?

Knowledge Building (KB)	Knowledge Object (KO)

☒ RESTORING:

Have the original structure surface and kept as much as possible.

☒ RESTRUCTURING:

Have the original structure surface to be completed and expanded and refunctionalized.

☒ REASSEMBLING:

Have the original shape surface as to have as many original parts and pieces fit together accordingly.

☒ RECONFIGURING:

Have a background knowledge model available as to have a plausible new setting consistently organized.

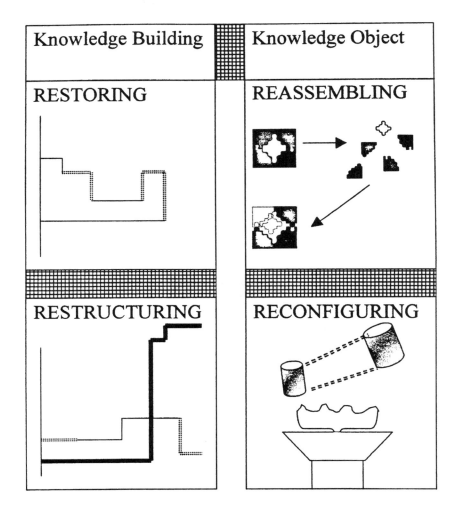

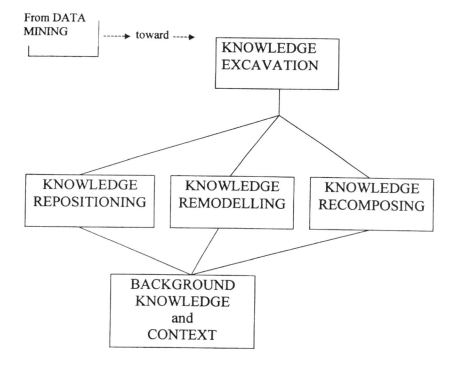

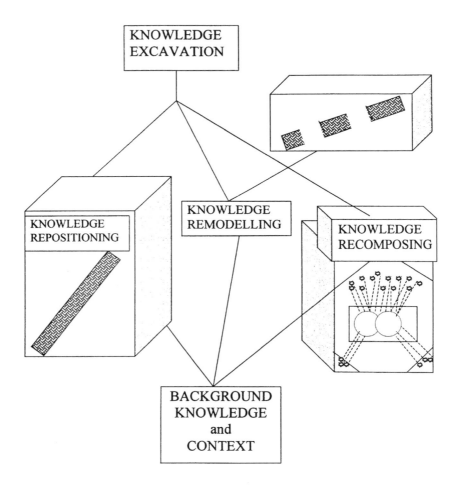

Information Design covers a whole variety of different problems in different fields.

This is why a global and "on top" competence is required as well as specific training meant to create a higher sensitivity within different information and communication environments.

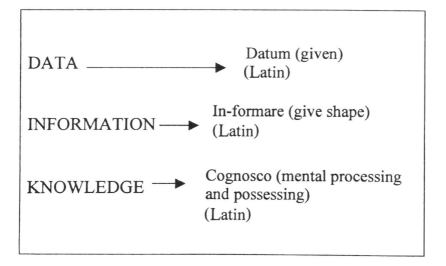

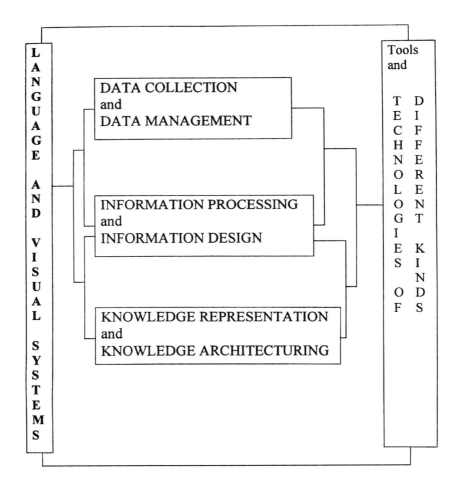

Leon Battista Alberti (1404-1472)

1. Knowledge about the different kinds of materials and their uses;

2. Implementation and execution of plans, which may respond to specific requests;

3. Beauty coming out of harmony as the absolute priority task to be achieved.

"The architect is a creative operator able to organize the setting problem considering and combining a various and wide set of differing parameters, sometimes contradictory as well. Architecture being the management of complexity".

From Gilbert Luigi "L'architecture en Europe", 1995, Editions Nathan, Paris

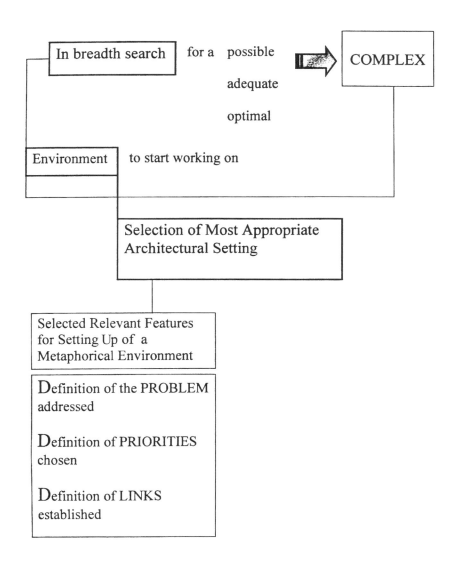

Metaphorical Environments
are based upon prospective knowledge building: they
anticipate in fact comprehensive mental models and pictures
for something to come (Latin: prospicere).

The process of metaphorical environment planning and
designing does, therefore, radically differ from any
retrospective model of analogical thinking (Latin:
retrospicere) based on surveying and re-using past events or
experiences.

"Retrospective thinking" is related to efficacy in prior time.

"Prospective thinking" is meant to be proactive therefore
serving to prepare for or intervene in or monitor an expected
occurrence or situation.

Metaphorical Environment Planning and Designing

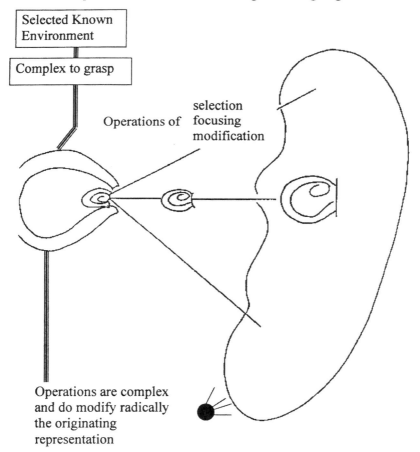

Selected Known
Environment

Complex to grasp

Operations of　selection
focusing
modification

Operations are complex
and do modify radically
the originating
representation

Lexical items transport is subject to the same rules and undergoes a complex process of redefinition

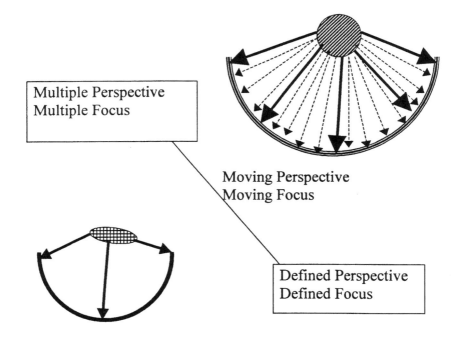

Multiple Perspective
Multiple Focus

Moving Perspective
Moving Focus

Defined Perspective
Defined Focus

Comments: The same metaphorical environment may generate differently evolving analogical processes at the same time or at different times. It is absolutely important to previously think and decide whether it is in fact really good to use the same metaphorical environment for different purposes, because the same model of reference may cause some confusion and misunderstanding.

It may be better to create a new and fully dedicated metaphorical environment to enlighten different perspectives. Some distance and distinctiveness principles may in fact serve to avoid collision and collapsing in interpretation processes.

Metaphorical Environment relevant features selection has to be based upon "in breadth" first and "in depth" next SEARCH.

In depth search is most important for ensuring accuracy in meaning creation.

Preciseness represents a fundamental aspect to establish sound criteria after some intuition and guessing have occurred.

Prospective Analogies are meant to visualize facts, events and elements in the process of being defined or redefined. Metaphorical Environments for Information Design represent the process of planning/thinking/rethinking/interpreting highly complex and dynamically articulated problems.

Levels of <u>approximation</u> required need to be first

<u>set – defined – monitored</u>

so as to be able to <u>work out the details</u> accordingly

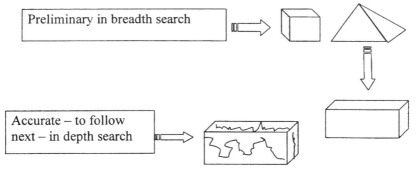

Preliminary in breadth search

Accurate – to follow
next – in depth search

Real insight for problem solution comes from both "in breadth" and "in depth" search processes.

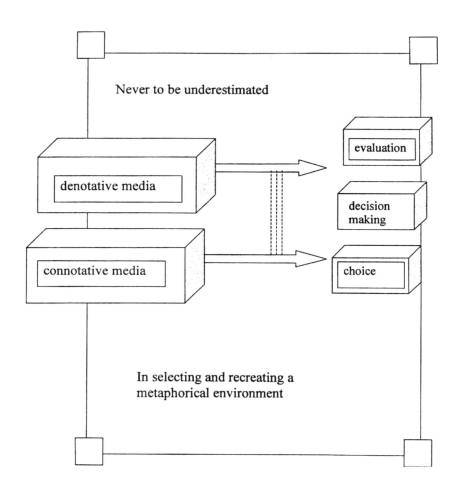

Metaphorical Environments
are based upon selection processes

The originating environment behind those very specific
features selected is there and visibly recognizable as soon as
triggered back.

"Information States" contains main examples of such
processes.

From an originating environment a selection of relevant
features is made as to proceed to further abstraction.

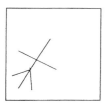

Once the originating environment is gone,
traces are visible through an accurate
description and explanation, to be made
surface progressively.

An enhanced metaphorical environment: Gaudí's
Architectural Models and Buildings

Gaudí has intentionally enhanced and extremized some very
specific aspects and features of Middle Ages Architecture after
having analyzed carefully the original models in all their
characteristics.

Gaudí has then focused on
                              pinnacles
                              lights
                              stones

By exaggerating, enhancing, zooming, multiple perspective
viewing, focusing and refocusing and mixing harmoniously other
traditions too.

Gaudí has in fact reproduced nature and motion out of the Catalan
tradition; including perception of Sardana dancing.

Final effect is therefore
                              reproduction
                              by
                              extremization

                              - though basic laws of balancing
                              are kept even in the most extreme
                              cases -

The reading and recognizing of the style/styles to be reproduced is possible through knowledge about the original style/styles in its/their characteristics and main features.

Like in the enhanced model of vision (the Gropius chair) multiple viewing is promoted.

Once the concept is well understood, because carefully explained and thoroughly illustrated in all its details any project (like Sagrada Familia) may be collectively completed according to "the special way of looking" meant to be promoted, once the project was first initiated.

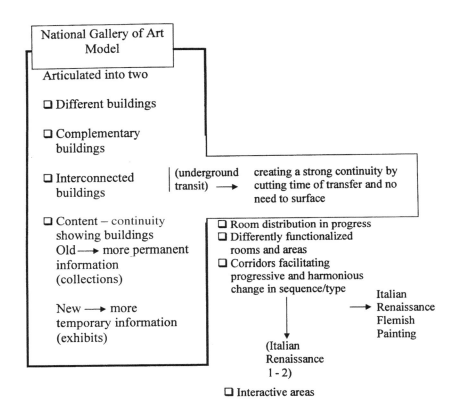

National Gallery of Art Model

Articulated into two

❑ Different buildings

❑ Complementary
   buildings

❑ Interconnected
   buildings

(underground transit) ⟶ creating a strong continuity by cutting time of transfer and no need to surface

❑ Content – continuity
   showing buildings
   Old ⟶ more permanent
   information
   (collections)

   New ⟶ more
   temporary information
   (exhibits)

❑ Room distribution in progress
❑ Differently functionalized
   rooms and areas
❑ Corridors facilitating
   progressive and harmonious
   change in sequence/type

⟶ Italian Renaissance Flemish Painting

(Italian Renaissance 1 - 2)

❑ Interactive areas

1. Access to packaged knowledge referring to more general knowledge (ARTSHOP)
2. Discussion and conversation area for information passing and knowledge distribution (COFFEEHOUSE)

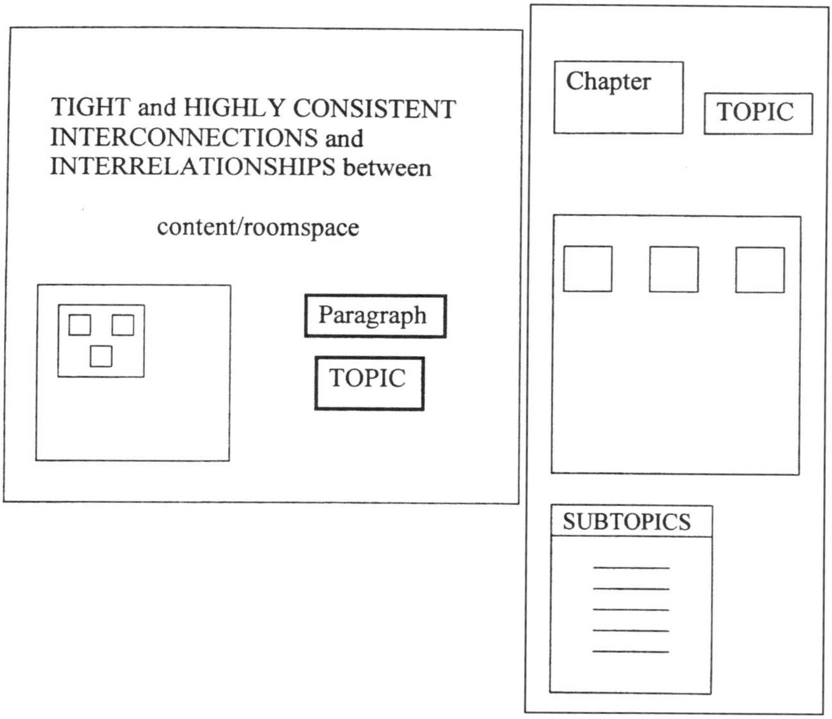

TIGHT and HIGHLY CONSISTENT
INTERCONNECTIONS and
INTERRELATIONSHIPS between

content/roomspace

Paragraph

TOPIC

Chapter

TOPIC

SUBTOPICS

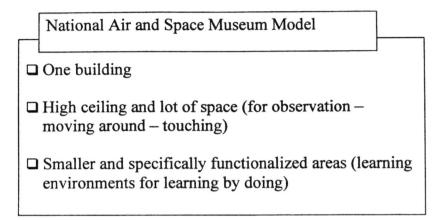

National Air and Space Museum Model

❑ One building

❑ High ceiling and lot of space (for observation – moving around – touching)

❑ Smaller and specifically functionalized areas (learning environments for learning by doing)

Need to focus – observe – analyze carefully a limited set of complex objects

Need to be helped in learning

Theater: collective learning
           perceptual experience

Exhibits: interactive learning both
           individually and collectively
           organized

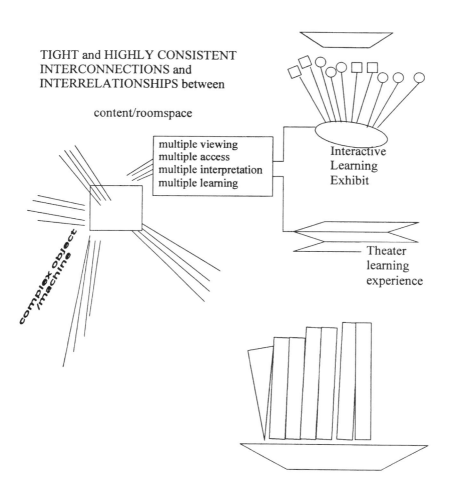

TIGHT and HIGHLY CONSISTENT
INTERCONNECTIONS and
INTERRELATIONSHIPS between

content/roomspace

multiple viewing
multiple access
multiple interpretation
multiple learning

complex object/machine

Interactive
Learning
Exhibit

Theater
learning
experience

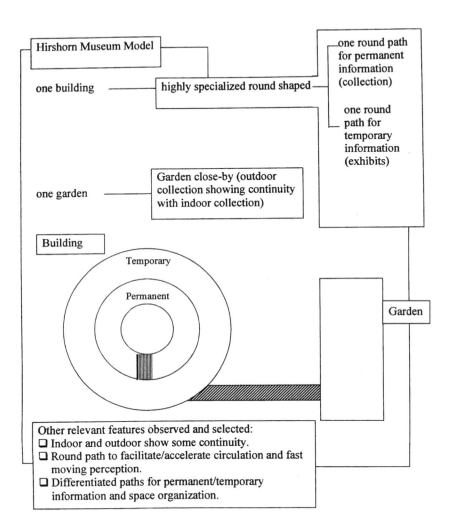

TIGHT and HIGHLY
CONSISTENT
INTERCONNECTIONS and
INTERRELATIONSHIPS between

content/roomspace/building/garden

specialized viewing
fast viewing

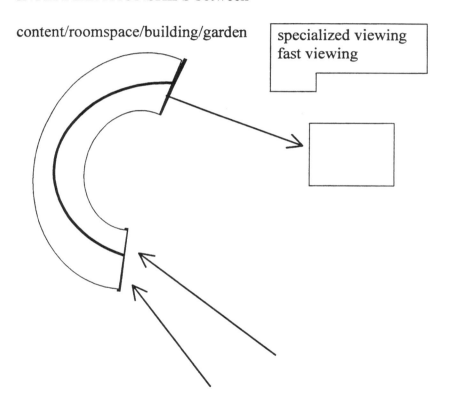

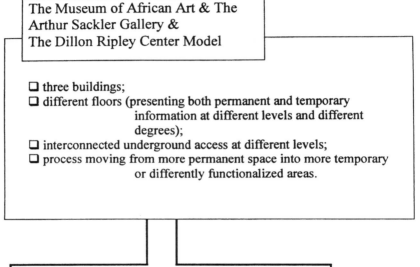

The Museum of African Art & The
Arthur Sackler Gallery &
The Dillon Ripley Center Model

❑ three buildings;
❑ different floors (presenting both permanent and temporary
        information at different levels and different
        degrees);
❑ interconnected underground access at different levels;
❑ process moving from more permanent space into more temporary
        or differently functionalized areas.

The progressive order of access is a powerful
metaphor for rethinking of different levels of
knowledge and information starting from the most
consolidated and stabilized one proceeding toward
more temporary and dynamically changing and
subject to update and revision one.

TIGHT and HIGHLY CONSISTENT
INTERCONNECTIONS and
INTERRELATIONSHIPS between

content/roomspace/buildings/levels of access

Key to African Art Museum Levels:

Ground Level: Level 1:   Level 2:   Level 3:
General Information   Exhibitions   Exhibitions   Access to S. Dillon
Pavilion   Access to Arthur   Ripley Center
                                        Sackler Gallery

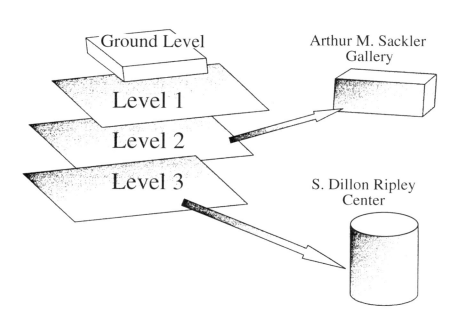

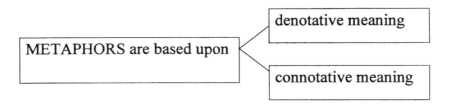

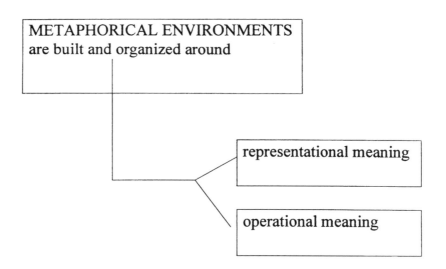

References

Biddle, D. S., Milne, A. K., and Shortle, D. A. 1974. *The Language of Topographic Maps.* Melbourne: The Jacaranda Press.

Chomsky, N. 1957. *Syntactic Structures.* The Hague: Mouton.

De Beaugrande, R. A., and Dressler, W. 1981. *Einfuhrung in die Textlinguistik.* Tubigen: Max Niemeyer Verlag.

Friedman, K. 1997. *Design Science and Design Education.* Norwegian School of Management, Research Report Series. Oslo: Norwegian School of Management.

Hobbs, J. R. 1985. Granularity. *Proceedings,* Ninth International Joint Conference on Artificial Intelligence, Los Angeles, California (August 1985): 432–35. Republished in *Readings in Qualitative Reasoning about Physical Systems,* edited by Daniel S. Weld and Johan de Kleer. San Mateo, Calif.: Morgan Kaufmann Publishers Inc., 1989.

Hollis, R. 1994. Graphic Design. London: Thames and Hudson.

Lehnert, W. G. 1981. Plot Units and Narrative Summarization. *Cognitive Science* 2: 293–331.

Levi, J. and Salvadori, M. 1987. *Why Buildings Fall Down.* New York: Norton.

Marchionini, G. 1995. *Information Seeking in Electronic Environments.* New York: Cambridge University Press.

Minsky, M. 1975. A Framework for Representing Knowledge. In *The Psychology of Computer Vision,* edited by P. H. Winston. New York: McGraw-Hill.

——— 1986. *The Society of Mind.* New York: Simon and Schuster.

Perkins, D. 1994. *The Intelligent Eye: Learning to Think by Looking at Art.* Los Angeles: The Getty Trust Publications.

Salvadori, M. 1980. *Why Buildings Stand Up.* New York: Norton.

Schank, R. C. 1972. Conceptual Dependency: A Theory of Natural Language Understanding. *Cognitive Psychology* 3 (4): 552–631.

——— 1980. Language and Memory. *Cognitive Science* 4 (3): 243–84.

Schriver, K. A. 1997. *Dynamics in Document Design: Creating Texts for Readers.* New York: John Wiley and Sons.

Sless, D. 1978. *Visual Thinking.* Adelaide: Adelaide University.

Tonfoni, G. 1988. Percezione concettuale del testo e processi direzionati di riassunto (Text conceptual perception and summarization goal-oriented processes). In *Atti del XIX Congresso Internazionale della Società Linguistica Italiana su "Dalla parte del ricevente: percezione, comprensione, interpretazione,"* 8–10 novembre 1985, edited by T. De Mauro, S. Gensini, and M. E. Piemontese. Roma: Bulzoni.

——— 1990. *Text Representation Systems.* Helsinki: Eurographica Oy.

—————— 1990. *La lettura strategica. Tecniche cognitive per leggere di più e meglio* (Strategic reading: Cognitive techniques to read more and better), with G. Tassi. Milano: Mondadori Informatica.

—————— 1991. La scrittura multimediale: Tecniche di progettazione e design testuale (Multimedia writing: Textual design and architecturing). Treviso: Pagus.

—————— 1991. La communicazione aziendale come arte visiva (Business communication as visual art). Treviso: Pagus.

—————— 1991. Didattica del testo: Curricolo di formazione linguistica per gli insegnanti (Teaching through texts: The teacher's guide to text writing and reading). Teramo: Giunti e Lisciani.

—————— 1991. Sistemi cognitivi complessi (Complex cognitive systems). Treviso: Pagus.

—————— 1991. Communicative cooperative interaction models: gap-filling processes by reformulation. In *Referate der Dritten Arbeitstagung Dialoganalyse III,* 1990, Bologna, edited by S. Stati, E. Weigand, and F. Hundsnurscher. Tubigen: Max Niemeyer Verlag.

—————— 1991. Traduzione e sistemi di rappresentazione della conoscenza (Translation and knowledge representation systems), in *Koinè, Annali della Scuola Normale Superiore per Interpreti e Traduttori,* 1991, 1 (2): 33–56.

—————— 1991. Linguaggio come arte visiva: Sistemi di rappresentazione del testo (Language and Visual Art: Text Representation Systems), in Atti del XII Festival International de la Video et des Artes Electroniques-Tavola Rotonda, settembre 1991, Locarno.

—————— 1992. Partitura solfeggio, movimento: Note di esecuzione di scrittura (Partitioning, sol-fa, movement: Notes on execution of writing). Treviso: Pagus.

—————— 1992. Traduzione e science cognitive: sistemi di reppresentazione del testo (Translation and cognitive sciences: Text representation systems), in Atti della Fiera Internazionale della Traduzione, 10–12 dicembre 1990, Riccione, 57–73, Forlì, Ateneo Editrice.

—————— 1992. Processi di autoriflessione cognitiva ed apprendimento: Laboratorio di multimedialità attiva e tecniche di visualizzazione dei percorsi di traduzione dei testi (Cognitive self-reflection processes and learning: Active multimedia laboratory and visualization technique of text translation processes), in Atti del Convegno su "Il computer nell'apprendimento e nell'autoapprendimento linguistico," 11–12 ottobre 1991, Bologna, edited by R. Rossini Favretti, 77–84, Bologna: Monduzzi.

—————— 1992. Cognitive training and teaching support systems in artificial intelligence: On language and reasoning. *Settentrione* 3: 22–29.

—————— 1992. Dalla rappresentazione della conoscenza alla 'scienza della conoscenza': Sistemi di rappresentazione del testo (From knowledge representation to 'knowledge science': Text representation systems), in Calcolatori e scienze umane. Archeologia e arte, scienze giuridiche e sociali, linguistica, letteratura. Scritti del convegno organizzato dall' Accademia Nazionale dei Lincei e dalla Fondazione IBM Italia, 315–318, Milano: Etaslibri.

—————— 1992. Intelligenza artificiale: da un modello communicativo 'chiuso' a un sistema 'aperto' di gestione e revisione dell'implicito nelle conversazioni a scopo collaborativo (Artificial intelligence: From a 'closed' communicative model to an 'open' system for managing and revising 'implicit knowledge' in cooperative conversation), in La Linguistica Pragmatica, Atti del XXIV Congresso, 415–429, Roma: Bulzoni.

———— 1992. Modelli di rappresentazione lessicale per un ambiente multimediale (Lexical representation models for a multimedia environment), in Atti del Seminario Internazionale di Studi sul Lessico, 2–5 aprile 1992, Forlì-San Marino, Bologna: Clueb.

———— 1992. La multimedialità attiva (Active multimedia). *Media Duemila* 10 (7): 67–73.

———— 1993. Applicazioni della metodologia CPP-TRS in ambiente didattico (Applications of CPP-TRS methodology to a teaching environment). *Informatica e Scuola* 2 (January): 26–29.

———— 1993. Produrre multimedialità (Multimedia production). *Media Duemila* 11 (2): 27–29.

———— 1993. Il disegno multimediale (Multimedia drawing). *Media Duemila* 11 (4): 78–80.

———— 1994. CPP-TRS: On Using Visual Cognitive Symbols to Enhance Communication Effectiveness. Paper presented at ISMCR-94: Topical Workshop on Virtual Reality, Fourth International Symposium on Measurement and Control in Robotics, NASA, Houston, Texas, Nov. 30–Dec. 3; Library of Congress #94-69310.

———— 1994. *Writing as a Visual Art*, Exeter: Intellect first abridged English version (with J. Richardson and with a foreword by Marvin Minsky).

———— 1994. *Frammenti testuali* [Textual Fragments], Parma: Zara.

———— 1994. La metodologia CPP-TRS per l'interazione uomo-macchina (The CPP-TRS methodology for man-machine interaction). *AEI-Automazione Energia Informazione* 81 (6): 69–74.

———— 1994. A dynamic model for representing invisible aspects of language. In *Atti del IV Convegno dell'Associazione Italiana per l'Intelligenza Artificiale, Atti del gruppo di lavoro su "Aspetti Espistemologici e Gnoseologici dell'Intelligenza Artificiale,* edited by M. Somalvico. Parma: Università di Parma.

———— 1995a. *Abitare il Testo* [Living in Text], Treviso: Pagus.

———— 1995b. CPP-TRS: On Using Visual Cognitive Symbols to Enhance Communication Effectiveness, ISMCR-94: International Symposium on Measurement and Control in Robotics, NASA, Houston, November 30–December 3, 1994, Library of Congress, 94-69310, Washington, D.C.

———— 1995c. A visual language for representing invisible aspects of natural language. *Intelligent Tutoring Media* 6 (2): 84–90.

———— 1996a. *Communicative Patterns and Textual Forms*. Exeter: Intellect.

———— 1996b. A visual news processing environment. *Artificial Intelligence Review* 10 (3–4): 187–208.

More information is available at http://www.intellect-net.com/authors/tonfoni.htm and at http://www.cirfid.unibo.it/project/ile and at http://www.ideography.co.uk/idn98/

Tufte, E. R. 1990. *Envisioning Information*. Cheshire, Conn.: Graphics Press.

————. 1991. *The Visual Display of Quantitative Information*. Cheshire, Conn.: Graphics Press.

Weeks, M. E. (completed by H. M. Leicester). 1968. Discovery of the Elements. *Journal of Chemical Education*.

Wilensky, R. 1983. *Planning and Understanding.* Reading, Mass.: Addison-Wesley.
Winston, P. H. 1982. Learning New Principles from Precedents and Exercises. *Artificial Intelligence* 19: 321–50.

A very important source of information and reference to the literature and tradition of Information Design is the Information Design Association in the U.K.

Available sources made available by IdeAs and expertly coordinated by Conrad Taylor:
http://www.popcomm.co.uk/ida/IDA.html
http://www.ideography.co.uk/idn98/

Index

About the Author

Dr. Graziella Tonfoni, who has been Research Professor of Computational Linguistics at the University of Bologna, Italy, has conceived and written this book while being a visiting scholar at the College of Library and Information Services, University of Maryland, College Park. She is internationally known for her contributions to textual theory, cognitive science, artificial intelligence, communications, training, and multimedia education. She has also been a visiting scholar at MIT and at Harvard University and has presented her methodology in many U.S. universities and research centers.